Building a Nation

Building a Nation

A HISTORY OF THE AUSTRALIAN HOUSE

JOHN ARCHER

COLLINS

AUSTRALIA

ACKNOWLEDGMENTS

This book was commissioned by the Australian Bicentennial
Authority in 1985 but many others have contributed to its creation.
I would like to thank the staff of the:
Australian Archives (Melbourne, Canberra, Darwin)
Australian Museum, Sydney
Forestry Commission of Victoria
Fryer Library, Brisbane University
John Oxley Library, State Library of Queensland
J.S. Battye Library of West Australian History, Perth
Latrobe Collection, State Library of Victoria
Macleay Museum, Sydney
Mitchell Library, State Library of NSW
Museum of Victoria
National Library of Australia, Canberra
New England Historical Resources Centre, Armidale
Powerhouse Museum, Sydney
Promotion Australia
Social History Museum, Deakin University
State Library of South Australia
State Library of Tasmania
And the various regional historical societies throughout Australia.

Of the individuals who gave so freely of their time, energy and expertise, I am especially grateful to the following:
Ian Evans, Rod Fisher, Peter Newell, Norman Day, Peter McIntyre, Sir Albert Jennings, Ian Fox, George Palmer,
Adrian Welke and Phil Harris of Troppo Architects, Peter Forrest, Norman C. Ireland, Evan McGilvray, Jock
Elphwick, and Gail Margieson who typed the manuscript.

Finally, I would like to express my gratitude to Tom Tomson and Richard Smart for their belief in the book's original
concept, and to my partner Linda Moyle whose patience, assistance, and encouragement helped to make it possible.

This publication has been partially funded by The Australian Bicentennial Authority to celebrate Australia's Bicentenary in 1988.

© John Archer 1987
First published by William Collins Pty Ltd Sydney 1987

Produced by Jackie Gaff & Steven Dunbar
Edited by Carson Creagh
Index by Dianne Regtop
Typeset by John Shute ASA Typesetters Sydney
Printed by Griffin Press Adelaide

National Library of Australia
Cataloguing-in-Publication data

Archer, John, 1941–
Building a nation.

Bibliography.
Includes index.
ISBN 0 00 217498 7.

1. Architecture, Domestic — Australia — History.
I. Title.

728.3'0994

Photograph on page 5 courtesy the J.S. Battye Library of West Australian History
Photograph on page 8 courtesy the Latrobe Collection, State Library of Victoria

Contents

Introduction

*A culture begins with the simple things — with the way the potter moulds
the clay on his wheel, the way a weaver threads his yarns, the way the builder builds his house.
Greek culture did not begin with the Parthenon: it began with a white-washed hut on a hillside.*
Herbert Read *The Politics of the Unpolitical* 1943

Originating somewhat later than the Greeks', Australian architecture began in 1788 with the first collection of hastily built whitewashed huts around Sydney Cove. Australian culture, however, began fifty thousand years or more ago.

Beginning with an examination of traditional Aboriginal house forms, this book investigates the two hundred years of transition from the convict hut to the modern suburban home. It is not intended to be an orthodox architectural history — quite the reverse.

Most historical accounts begin with 'primitive' huts and progress rapidly to the work of colonial architects such as Francis Greenway, John Verge and John Lee Archer, whose grand and imposing mansions have little in common with the houses most people lived in at the time. In a similar fashion, the modern architecture featured in glossy magazines often bears little resemblance to life in the suburbs.

It has been argued by some that architectural style begins with the expression of avant-garde architects and filters down to the greater mass of society. In theory, then, this elite group deserves our special attention, because it represents the major creative impetus in housing — albeit a delayed and indirect input. The 'classic' approach is bound to have a heavy social bias; urban and architectural philosopher Bernard Rudofsky once commented that this form of architectural history 'amounts to little more than a who's who of architects who commemorated power and wealth; an anthology of buildings of, by, and for the privileged ... with never a word about the houses of lesser people'.

Building a Nation is dedicated to the anonymous houses of those lesser mortals — the people responsible for creating the homes of ordinary Australians, the greater proportion of our built environment.

Robin Boyd described such architecture as a material triumph and an aesthetic calamity. Ugliness, like beauty, is very much in the eye of the beholder; I would rather make no such judgment, and prefer to see houses simply as the shells in which we create our lives.

The houses we remember with the most affection are usually those in which we were happy, rather than those with particular aesthetic or architectural merit, and the architect who can design such a home is an alchemist indeed. The truth is that whether we design or build them ourselves, choose them or find ourselves occupying them by force of circumstance, our houses remain shells until we inhabit them and give them character and life. For this reason I have selected where possible photographs that show house and occupants together, rather than the more sterile views of the traditional architectural style.

These photographs are the result of a long-standing obsession with such images. During the past ten years I have been collecting copies of early photographs of people and their houses from a vast network of sources. The collection soon began to fill filing-cabinet drawers. At the same time I kept aside first-person accounts or contemporary descriptions of homes and their surroundings, hoarding them as a collector does rare stamps. This material provided the basis on which to build, and a grant from the Australian Bicentennial Authority assisted by funding further research.

Considerable thought was necessary before a decision was reached on the most appropriate form in which to present the material. As a sculptor I have always been attracted by the concept of the assemblage: the careful combination of small found objects to produce a large finished work, where the artist's skill lies in the selection and placing of each piece.

Building a Nation is an assemblage of description and image, the story of the evolution of our homes told by those who witnessed or participated in that evolution.

During its preparation I have been constantly grateful for the work of earlier historians, whose books have provided a continual source of inspiration and information; in particular Professor J.M. Freeland's *Architecture in Australia*, Robin Boyd's *Australia's Home* and, more recently, Ian Evans' *The Australian Home* and *The Federation House*.

Of all these it was Robin Boyd's well-thumbed and now disintegrating volume that was my most consistent companion. In 1952 Boyd wrote that 'the small house, probably more than anything else that man has done, has made the face of Australia and to an extent the faces of Australians'.

Here are the voices and the faces of some of those Australians.
This is their book.

John Archer
Brunswick Heads 1987

'No Permanent Habitations'

FOR THOUSANDS OF YEARS PRIOR TO EUROPEAN occupation, Australia was a land of great cultural diversity. Languages, customs and technology varied considerably as Aboriginal people developed appropriate responses to the regions in which they settled. Nowhere is this more obvious than in their dwellings.

In his book *Natives of Australia,* written at the turn of the century, N.W. Thomas compiled a series of descriptions of Aboriginal houses extracted from the accounts of early explorers and anthropologists:

The Australian native is commonly represented as possessing no permanent habitation; hardly anything, in fact, which can be called a hut. This is not even true of Victoria, still less of the natives of northerly districts, who found themselves in need of protection against the rain more than the natives of the south needed shelter from the cold of winter. The prevailing type in the south is or was the bark hut or rather breakwind, formed by sheets of bark arched over, or by boughs or both. This afforded little shelter, but the open side was turned round so that it was away from the wind, thus sheltering the fire, which stood on the same side and allowing the wind to drive the smoke away ...

On the Hutt River, Grey found more substantial dwellings still, evidently intended for permanent habitation, for in the neighbourhood were large yam grounds; this was one of the few areas in which anything like real cultivation of the ground was found among the Aborigines. The huts were larger and plastered over with clay and sods.

In the direction of Hanover Bay, Grey found an even better type: it was built of logs of wood, in shape like a beehive, about four feet high and nine feet in diameter. Probably the huts found by Peron at Shark's Bay were of this type; they were sixteen feet long and carpeted with seaweed; in the walls were recesses for storing implements, the entrances were about three feet high.

Somewhat similar huts were in use in Victoria. Eyre found a village of thirteen huts near Mount Napier, they were cupola-shaped, made of a strong wood frame covered with thick turf, the grassy sides inwards. Some were semicircular, some had two entrances, one was ten feet by fifteen, and so strong that a man could ride over it. At Port Fairy similar erections were found, some large enough for twelve people, and higher than most of the native huts; they were six feet high and had a floor of bark.

In the roof was an aperture nine inches in diameter for the smoke to escape, which in wet weather was covered with a sod. Were it not that this information was received from an early settler, it would be probable that the natives had profited by European example; as it is, the type is not so far removed from those already described that a foreign origin must necessarily be ascribed to these Port Fairy huts.

Facing page
The tepee-like bark shelters of this 'Native Encampment' (illustrated by John Skinner Prout in the 1840s) provided shelter from both wind and rain, and were kept warm by small fires.
MITCHELL LIBRARY

13

Two types of shelter can be seen in this photograph of an Aboriginal camp in northern Queensland. Building the leaf-and-bark 'beehive' (right) would have taken just a few minutes.
MITCHELL LIBRARY

The highest type of all . . . was found by King at Careening Bay. It was situated on a hill, and formed of two walls of stone, three feet high, with saplings across at each end, thatched with bark and grass, but we cannot be certain that it was not built by Europeans or Malays. Other authors, however, describe circular stone erections in North-West Australia.

Of a different type from the Port Fairy huts, but equally permanent, were those seen by Eyre at White Lake in Latitude 36°40'. These were circular, made of straight rods meeting at a central upright pole; the outside was first covered with bark and grass, then coated with clay. The fire was in the centre and the smoke hole was made in the roof. On the Gwydir, Mitchell saw another type of a slighter construction, but remarkable for having a conical roof with a portico on one side supported on two sticks.

Collins describes a hut at Shoal Bay made of vine tendrils crossing each other lashed with wiry grass. The walls were of Melaleuca bark and the hut

was weatherproof; it was eight feet in diameter, and four and a half feet high, the entrance was by a small avenue with a turn in it and fires were lighted inside. One was large enough for fifteen persons.

At Moreton Bay another type was found, formed of three sticks meeting at the top, which were covered with Melaleuca bark. It was only large enough for one family, and they slept in a semicircular position on bark, covering themselves with skins. Somewhat similar are the Boulia district huts described by Roth. Bent saplings are fixed in the earth, and the tops interlocked at a height of four feet or more; against these lean secondary sticks and the interstices are filled with light brushes and grass; over this comes another layer of bushes; they are circular and sometimes have two entrances.[1]

Few observers were as perceptive as Thomas and, since the diversity of materials and styles was not obvious, they often assumed in their ignorance

Above: with its soft floor of grass and fern, this paperbark gunyah at Port Macquarie, NSW, was a comfortable temporary shelter for a trio of Aboriginal hunters.
THOMAS DICK *c*1910, AUSTRALIAN MUSEUM

Left: These bark-and-brush shelters were 'captured' by French miner and photographer Antoine Fauchery in 1858 when travelling in the Gippsland region of Victoria.
LATROBE LIBRARY

Photographed at the turn of the century, a dome-shaped spinifex shelter is surrounded by shade areas (wiltjas) which provide some relief from the fierce sun of north-western Australia.
BATTYE LIBRARY

that the particular house form they saw was common to an entire race. The nomadic behaviour and casual approach of Aborigines to material things such as houses also shocked the English. Sir Joseph Banks noted from the comfort of the *Endeavour*:

Naked as these people are when abroad they are scarce at all better defended from the injuries of the weather when at home, if that name can with propriety be given to their houses — as I believe

they never make any stay in them but wandering like the Arabs from place to place set them up whenever they meet with one where sufficient supplys of food are to be met with, and as soon as these are exhausted remove to another leaving the houses behind, which are framd with less art or rather less industry than any habitations of human beings probably that the world can shew.[2]

Robert Gouger, writing in South Australia in 1837, was equally dismissive:

The natives have no settled place of abode, but each family wanders over a space of several miles, an aggression upon which by another family is invariably punished. And they have no fixed habitations; when the family, either from vicinity to the grubs or other strong inducement, determines to settle for a time upon a particular spot, they pull down some branches of trees, and construct a few huts about four feet high and in the form of a bee-hive cut in half: they are thus quite open on one side, and here at night they keep a large fire.[3]

Although many tribal groups in Central Australia's deserts built shelters of the type described by Gouger, it was by no means as simple or random an act as it appeared. Considerable skill and traditional lore are involved, as Noel Wallace's description of Pitjantjatjara shelters illustrates:

The two traditional shelters of an Aboriginal camp are the yu (windbreak) and the wiltja (literally, shade). As their names imply, one is protection from the wind, the other is protection from the heat of the sun. Neither in itself is a dwelling (for example, neither provides much protection in its original form from rain, when a fire for warmth suffices). The fire, not the yu or wiltja, symbolises the place of dwelling.

Nor were the yu or wiltja a home — a place in which to keep and protect possessions. The yu or wiltja does not equate to a house. It is not a primitive house, but is an adequate structure which provides certain kinds of protection from the elements and which has always been an integral part of traditional life. An Aboriginal's 'home' is the outdoors, his tribal land.

After European missions and settlements appeared, camps were usually located in a wooded area, near water (spring, rockhole or bore) and dry firewood. Traditional wiltjas were built from stout tree branches, covered thickly and expertly with brush and spinifex, the only evidence of European influence being tarpaulin covers to make them more weatherproof. The earth inside was dish-shaped with the rim within the outer walls to repel surface water. Cross pieces were omitted from side walls so that when the wind changed it was a matter of minutes to block up the existing doorway and provide a new one on the lee side. In addition, lack of solid walls made it easy to burst one's way through should it catch fire, a not uncommon occurrence.

The wall structure of leaves and spinifex allowed draught-free ventilation and egress for smoke from fires. In hot weather it was a matter of a few minutes to remove the roof and turn a wiltja into a yu.

It was also a simple matter to move the whole structure to a new location within the camp. Anyone who has spent time in a traditional camp situation will know that it is never static. Daily there is some movement and change to the location of some wiltjas. It used to be a simple matter also when, for any of a number of reasons, the whole camp had to move to a new site, to leave everything behind and erect wiltjas using entirely new materials. Wiltja-building material was in plentiful supply, and in very little time a new, clean, hygienic camp could be built.[4]

In most cases the gathering of the material and the building were done by the women although, it would seem, not without incident:

When a man has two wives many quarrels arise between them on those hut building occasions. We remember seeing a dispute between two ladies of one lord over the erection of a loondthal, which all the husband's marital authority failed to accommodate. It therefore culminated in a fair stand-up fight, yamsticks being the weapons used, and their method of using them is no child's play either, as they lay on with all their might; so in this instance broken and gory heads were soon visible. After a very fierce encounter one gave in beaten, and the construction of the loondthal went on to completion, after which, however, a wordy phase of the disagreement supervened, until their long tongues and vituperative expletives fairly roused the angry passions of their lord and master (who was seated between the dark-skinned combatants) till his

17

savage nature could no longer bear the infliction; therefore he jumped up and caught hold of the centre pole, to which he gave a sudden jerk, and thus let the whole fabric down on the heads of his rival dearies, thereby putting a climax to their clatter. Satisfied with the result so suddenly achieved, he walked off to a neighbouring loond-thal, where he passed the time in pleasant aboriginal gossip until his termagant helpmates had re-erected his dwelling and got rid of their bad blood, by means of the healthy and arduous occupation which their husband had so unceremoniously thrust upon them.[5]

In Northern Australia the heavy rains of the wet season, the intense heat, and the nuisance of mosquitos and sandflies led to the development of buildings that vary not just from area to area but from season to season. The abundance of food on the coast meant people could stay in one spot for longer and could therefore build more substantial and complex houses.

In the far north of Queensland, probably the most popular type of native dwelling is a circular grass-and-bark hut, which resembles in some respects the kraal of the African Zulu. It is easily and quickly made of curved branches so arranged that they form an interlaced network, over which grass and strips of bark are hung, and are tied in place with vines. Some of these huts measure up to thirty feet in diameter and seven feet in height in the centre. But along the Mitchell River on the western coast of the Cape York Peninsula, small huts of this type are built without any framework of branches; they are low, round huts resembling the igloos of the Esquimaux, and are built solely of sheets of bark and palm-leaves. The frail structures, which often collapse during storms or windy weather, will not accommodate more than two natives at a crush; they are rarely more than three feet in height in the middle, and the entrance is so low and so narrow that the natives are compelled to get down on their hands and knees and crawl into their tiny homes!

Small doorways are a noticeable feature of all aboriginal dwellings in the far north ... they are easy to close from the inside with a sheet of bark. The huts are always kept firmly closed at night, no matter how hot the weather may be, for most of the bush tribes are intensely superstitious, and they believe that an open hut is tempting the evil spirits, or 'ghosts', too much!

From time immemorial the aborigines in the far north have used mud extensively in building their primitive homes. Probably the largest native mud houses to be seen in the Commonwealth are in the Roper River district (Northern Territory). Many of the tribes in this district build huge, mud-plastered houses, which are constructed by fastening a stout ridge-pole between two adjacent trees or two poles sunk into the ground. Other poles are leaned against the ridge-pole from both sides, and these are covered with reeds and grass, and finally with wet clay, which is thoroughly plastered in and smoothed down by hand. These huts are often up to thirty feet in length and ten feet in width, and will accommodate two dozen natives with ease. A narrow doorway, about three feet high, is left in one end, the other being closed.

Queer mud huts, remarkably like the tepees of the North American Indians, are also built by some of the tribes living in the coastal areas of Arnhem Land. These are constructed by erecting poles or branches around about five-sixths of a circle, six feet or eight feet in diameter, and meeting at a point eight feet or ten feet above the ground. The bottoms of the poles are embedded in the ground, and they are securely tied with vines at the apex. The sides are made perfectly watertight by being plastered with a 'cement' made of a mixture of leaves, grass, and clayey mud. Loose sheets of bark are provided for a door.

Peculiar double-storied houses are built by some of the Cape York Peninsula tribes. The dwellings are built on the ground, and have a stout framework of saplings tied securely at the joints with vines. In most cases the walls and roof are of sheets of bark sewn together with animal sinews, but a few of the homes have roofs of thatched grass. The floor between the upper and lower rooms is of

Above: human ingenuity arrives at similar responses to similar problems across the world. This hut skeleton photographed in Queensland's Atherton district in the 1890s bears a striking resemblance to the huts built in tropical Africa and the jungles of South America.
JOHN OXLEY LIBRARY

Left: beneath their thatching of palm leaves, these 'Native Mia Mias' photographed near Ingham, north Qld, have skeletons as tight and strong as the cane baskets in the foreground.
JOHN RAY COLLECTION

Soft, pliable and easy to shape, the thick bark of the paperbark tree was used wherever it was available. Its many layers of porous fibre swell when wet to make a virtually watertight roof.
THOMAS DICK *c*1910, AUSTRALIAN MUSEUM

saplings covered with bark, and rarely are any of the rooms more than five feet or six feet in height. The upper room is usually the sleeping-place of the children, while the parents occupy the lower room.[6]

Aborigines used a wealth of natural materials — sticks, bark, leaves, rushes and reeds — and developed special techniques to increase the effectiveness of each building component. The thick, strong and waterproof bark of the stringybark tree was softened over a slow fire, which melted the sap and allowed the bark to be shaped into canoes and coffins or flattened into sheets for roofing. Paperbark was even more versatile, being useful for blankets, ground cloths and food wrappings, and as a building material.

The grasstree was another valuable resource:

In West Australia the huts were constructed in less than half an hour by a couple of women. They are usually of grasstree (Xanthorrhoea arborea), but paperbark (Melaleuca) was also used. On arriving on the camping ground, the women set to work to collect bundles of dead flowering stems, six or seven feet long, from the grasstrees in the neighbourhood. Then making holes in the ground with their yam-sticks, they planted the stems in them to a depth of some eight inches; the holes were larger at the bottom than at the top, and ten inches apart, in the form of a horseshoe, the heel being the doorway. The stems were made to converge, and on them were placed withered curled grasstree rushes, which were held in position by the hard pointed

Above: some shelters were used solely for special purposes. This grass hut near the Tully River, north Qld, was used only for scarification ceremonies.
AUSTRALIAN MUSEUM

Left: although it looks fragile, this shelter of cabbage-tree palm leaves at Princess Charlotte Bay, Qld, protected its inhabitants both from heavy tropical rain and from the heat of the sun.
AUSTRALIAN MUSEUM

The destruction of traditional Aboriginal society saw uneasy compromises between black and white ways of life. This beehive hut in South Australia is lined with cast-off milled timber.
ROBERT JAMES COLLECTION

seed vessels of the stems. The framework was now ready, and the women proceeded to gather bundles of green straight grasstree rushes; holding them under the left arm they threw them with the right hand at an angle of 45 degrees, so that when the sharp points stuck among the covering of dead rushes, the weight of the green stems caused them to bend down and remain in their places. The thatching was begun at the ground and continued up to the top, where a second layer was put on, to render the roof watertight. When the heat of the sun had been on it for a few hours, the roof settled down and became smooth; a third coating of rushes was then put on, and the roof was good for many months, only the top requiring to be renewed.[7]

This expertise in the selection and use of native materials was passed on by example to the early settlers, who seldom acknowledged the source. Victorian squatter Edward Curr was an exception, observing in 1886:

Having camped out a good deal in the bush, I do not hesitate to pronounce the bark hut of the Blacks the most comfortable shelter I have met with, where firewood is obtainable, and much preferable to a tent, which indeed in almost all weathers is miserable enough.[8]

Stringybark in particular became part of Australian building folklore and is still occasionally used for sheds and huts in parts of east Gippsland, where hundred-year-old bark structures survive.

Although they were happy to investigate and adapt Aboriginal technology to suit their needs, few Europeans realised that Aboriginal houses had (and still have) considerable symbolic significance. In Arnhem Land, for instance, the forked posts, cross-poles and bark sheets of the typical structure are regarded as sacred totemic objects; dwellings recur as themes in Aboriginal paintings, songs and stories, just as they do in European culture.

If architecture is the stage on which the events and dramas of daily life are enacted, then the style and form of houses become as much a part of the cultural fabric as music or art. As such they are not readily susceptible to change, as this story from eastern Arnhem Land, collected by anthropologist Joseph Reser, illustrates:

A Macassan by the noteworthy name of Noa came by boat to the Arnhem Land coast in the distant past. Noa's boat was loaded with all of the material goods of his culture, including tobacco, axes, rice and, significantly, Macassan dwellings. Noa liked the country he saw, pulled his boat up on the beach and started unloading the fruits of his technology. Some wild honey bees, who were Aboriginal ancestral spirits, noticed Noa unloading his boat and asked why he had come to their country. Noa responded that he thought it was a good country and that he would like to settle there. He then showed the ancestral spirits what he had brought with him, and told them that they could share these things in return for their country. The honey bees expressed little interest in the various goods and turned them down; they said they had their own stone axes, their own bush foods and their own quite comfortable dwellings. Noa was insistent and continued unloading his goods and setting up his camp. He refused to listen to the bees' entreaties that he should leave. The bees then stung Noa repeatedly, so that he gathered up his goods, got into his boat and pushed out to sea. Noa's boat sank some distance from shore; it can still be seen today, in the form of a rock.[9]

Unfortunately for the Aborigines, another group of intending settlers on the east coast was not to be so easily discouraged.

Sketched near Geelong in the autumn of 1854, existing low vegetation has been utilised in these bark-covered mia-mias to provide additional protection from draughts.
LATROBE LIBRARY

'Windows They Have None' 1788-1820

WHEN THE FIRST FLEET DROPPED ANCHOR AT Sydney Cove, Governor Phillip and his band of reluctant nation-builders looked out at one of the most beautiful natural harbours in the world — a perfect site for a city. The transition from wilderness to metropolis, however, was not easy.

As well as the 700 tents intended as shelter for the officers and convicts, Phillip brought with him a house prefabricated in England by one Nathan Smith. The five-roomed structure of timber and oiled cloth took three weeks to assemble and was immediately occupied by the grateful governor, who found to his dismay that 'the canvas house I am under [is] neither wind nor waterproof'.[1]

In London it had been confidently assumed that the necessary materials for building would be obtained easily from local resources and that convicts anxious to redeem themselves would provide the labour. It was easier said than done.

The tools brought from England were designed for use with European timbers, but Australian hardwoods such as the Sydney red gum were more difficult to work. Less than one tree in every dozen felled was useable; even then, axes, saws and chisels were broken and blunted. The planks that were obtained were not very useful and Phillip wrote in his first dispatch: 'The timber is well described in Captain Cook's voyage but unfortunately it has one very bad quality which puts us to great inconvenience; I mean the large gum tree which splits and warps.'[2]

A search of the hinterland located some forests of *Casuarina torulosa*, or she-oak, which Cook had said resembled the English pine. This was easier to saw and split into shingles and weatherboards, but since it is a small tree its useful timber was restricted to lengths of only about 3 metres. Groves of cabbage-tree palm were found in a bay near the mouth of the harbour, and soon:

the longboats of the ships in the cove were employed in bringing up cabbage-tree from the lower part of the harbour, where it grew in great abundance, and was found, when cut into proper lengths, very fit for the purpose of erecting temporary huts, the posts and plates of which being made of the pine of this country, and the sides and ends filled in with lengths of cabbage-tree, plastered over with clay, formed a very good hovel. The roofs were generally thatched with the grass of the gum-rush; some were covered with clay, but several of these failed, the weight of the clay and heavy rain soon destroying them.[3]

The posts and plates of she-oak were milled with a pit saw, a device that could still be seen in parts of Australia in the early 1900s. Like the pit saw, many of the tools and methods used for working timber, brickmaking and thatching had developed in Europe over many centuries. Before examining the early houses and their construction, a brief examination of the technology that helped shape them during the eighteenth and nineteenth

Facing page
A 1796 view of Brickfield Hill, on the road from Sydney to Parramatta, shows the typical first cottage built by most settlers. Brick barrows like that in the foreground are still in use today.
COLLINS *AN ACCOUNT*

25

centuries will give some idea of the problems faced by their builders.

A felled tree was sawn into appropriate lengths with a crosscut saw. Near the log a pit about 2 metres deep and up to 7 metres long was dug. Wooden rollers made out of small trees were placed across the pit, and the log was rolled out on them and chocked into place.

The sawyer used a piece of twine rubbed in charcoal to mark a line along the top of the log. The leading sawyer, known as the 'top notcher' or 'top dog', stood on top of the log to align the 2-metre-long saw while his unfortunate companion, the 'underdog', worked in the pit. The saw cut on the down stroke, so not only did the underdog provide the cutting power, he spent his day showered by sawdust in an airless hole, often up to his knees in water during wet weather — it was not a popular occupation. Many early settlers and convicts having a tough time of it found they could readily identify with this situation, and the underdog gradually became a typical Australian folk

hero, gamely struggling against an unpleasant reality.

An alternative to pit sawing involved using wedges to split the log into slabs or billets. These could in turn be split into thin palings or shingles with an ancient tool called a froe: a blade with a wedge-shaped profile attached at a 90°-angle to a wooden handle. The blade is driven into a billet of free-splitting timber with a wooden club or mallet, then twisted to prise out the paling (thus its alternative name of paling knife).

Brickmaking in Sydney began with the discovery of a bed of suitable clay at Brickfield Hill in April 1788, and traditional English technology was again employed to exploit it. The clay was roughly broken, mixed with water and 'pugged', or trampled into a sticky mess by bare-footed convicts.

The pressing demand for building materials meant the clay was allowed to soak for only a day or two rather than the two months desirable for maximum moisture penetration. Bricks were then moulded on wooden tables, each with a flat board

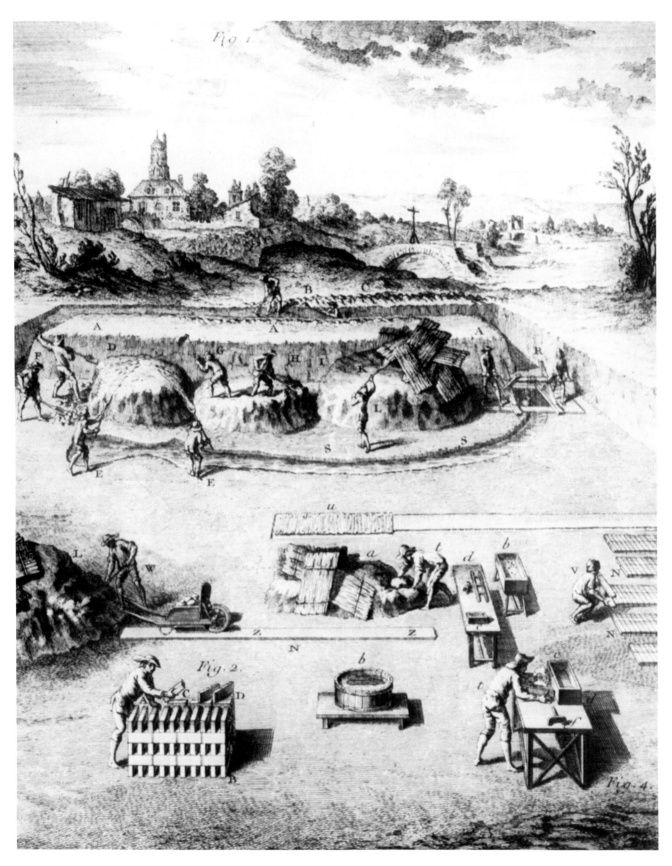

An eighteenth-century illustration of brick making shows techniques that were brought to Australia and used without substantial change until the advent of mechanisation.
DIDEROT'S ENCYCLOPAEDIA

27

Sketched just prior to its demolition in 1864, this simple cottage in a quiet Sydney street was built in 1791 and, according to legend, occupied at different times by governors Phillip and Bligh.
ILLUSTRATED SYDNEY NEWS

of heavy timber called a stock fixed on top. This was an anchor for the mould, which fitted over the top of the stock leaving space inside for the brick.

The first step in brickmaking was to dust the stock with sand; hence a 'sandstock' brick. Then the wet mould was slipped over the stock. It was filled with pugged clay packed in by hand and pushed well down into the corners with the brickmakers' thumbs (their imprints can often still be seen on handmade bricks). The top was levelled with a wooden bar, the mould removed, and the brick slipped along its sandy bed to a pallet.

The bricks were left to dry for a few days, then fired in wood-burning kilns. Unfortunately most of the early bricks were underfired, which gave them an attractive salmon colour but left them soft and porous. Gradually the quality of brick improved over the years and by 1870, when machinery replaced the handmaking process, hard and durable bricks were being manufactured all over Australia.

The first bricks and flat terracotta shingles were reserved for the governor, who at the last minute opted for a larger house than he had previously thought necessary: 'The house intended for myself

was to consist of only three rooms; but having a good foundation, has been enlarged, contains six rooms, and is so well built that I presume it will stand for a great number of years.'[4]

The huts of the lesser mortals were simple one-room affairs with wooden frames, drop log walls of cabbage palm plastered with clay, and roofs thatched with gum rushes (*Xanthorrhoea*, or grass-tree, leaves). Other rushes were harvested around the harbour, notably at Rushcutters Bay.

Openings in the walls for light and air were covered when necessary by woven shutters, described in a letter from an anonymous female convict in November 1788: 'Windows they have none, as from the Governor's house, etc, now nearly finished, no glass could be spared; so that lattices of twigs are made by our people to supply their places.'[5]

To make the process of hut building faster, cabbage-tree walling was replaced by wattle and daub, a building method common to most of Europe. Thin branches were woven into a series of vertical studs set into the wooden frame — this was known as wattlework — then coated with clay plaster or daub to provide a protective coating. Various species of *Acacia* were found to be ideal and became generally known as wattle trees. Fortunately they were in plentiful supply.

Such, then, were the possibilities that presented themselves to the aspiring builder desperate to upgrade from his rotting tent. Gradually, a settlement of simple attractive Georgian huts and cottages grew, with walls plastered in white pipeclay, and shingle roofs replacing the unsatisfactory thatch. A similar village developed at Parramatta, twenty-five kilometres inland, where the land seemed fertile enough for successful agriculture and unspoiled enough for an attempt at town planning:

The main street of the new town is already begun. It is to be a mile long, and of such a breadth as will make Pall Mall and Portland-Place 'hide their diminished heads'. It contains at present 32 houses completed, of 24 feet by 12 each, on a ground floor only, built of wattles plastered with clay, and thatched. Each house is divided into two rooms, in one of which is a fireplace and a brick chimney. These houses are designed for men only; and ten is the number of inhabitants allotted to each; but some of them now contain 12 or 14, for want of better accommodation. More are building; in a cross street stand nine houses for unmarried women — and exclusive of all these are several small huts where convict families of good character are allowed to reside.[6]

Lieutenant John Macarthur took up his first grant nearby, naming it Elizabeth Farm in honour of his wife, and with the help of ten assigned convicts built a large comfortable home in 1794:

In the centre of my farm I have built a most excellent brick house, 68 feet in front, and 18 feet in breadth. It has no upper storey, but consists of four rooms in the ground floor, a large hall, closets, cellar, etc.; adjoining is a kitchen, with servants' apartments and other necessary offices.[7]

One of the features of Elizabeth Farm was its spacious verandah. The verandah had been common in Spanish and Portuguese houses since med-

Top: in the 1790s twelve to fourteen convicts would have crowded into a wattle-and-daub hut like this. Often divided into two rooms, the cottage has an earth floor and window shutters of woven wattle.
JOHN ARCHER

Centre: glass was prohibitively expensive for most settlers, and windows were usually secured by shutters. This replica slab house, in Old Sydney Town, has neat wooden shutters and a roof of close-cropped thatch.
JOHN ARCHER

Bottom: a nineteenth-century botanist examines specimens of *Xanthorrhoea arborea*, the gum rush or grasstree that provided early settlers with durable thatching materials.
MITCHELL LIBRARY

Above: only fourteen years after the first tents and huts were erected for sea-weary soldiers and convicts, Sydney has the settled — even moderately prosperous — look of an established colony.
MITCHELL LIBRARY

Right: an imposing building when this painting was executed in the 1860s, John Macarthur's home, Elizabeth Farm, was one of the first buildings in Australia to incorporate extensive verandahs.
MITCHELL LIBRARY

iaeval times and appeared in their settlements in India and the West Indies. The British, noting the verandah's virtues in hot, humid and wet climates, copied the style in their Indian and North American colonies. Since the military forces were moved about from garrison to garrison around the world, it is hardly surprising that some of the officers of the New South Wales Corps were familiar with the concept.

In 1792 Lieutenant-Governor Robert Ross built the first verandah in Australia, along the entire frontage of his stone house, and similiar additions soon began to appear as their value in moderating the sun's heat on the walls of a building was realised. The verandah also provided an external access to rooms in larger houses, so that no hallway was necessary.

During the 1790s many of the settlement's first houses were replaced or upgraded. Immigrants and emancipated convicts began to build more comfortable cottages as bricks and lime mortar became more available; while joiners started to produce panelled doors and mullioned sliding windows from local red cedar for those who could afford them.

For those who could not, life was still tolerable. James Grant, visiting Sydney in 1800, noticed that by then most families had a home of their own, albeit a tiny one, which put them a long way ahead of their counterparts in Britain:

It is seldom that two families inhabit one dwelling, therefore every man becomes absolute master of his own house, and when he can afford it, he weatherboards and paints it. In the smallest dwelling I entered, I never saw less than two apartments. Many houses are constructed with bricks, and as well finished to the eye as European buildings; in such the apartments [sic] are numerous. In short, from the very comfortable manner these people are lodged (much more so than the poorer sort in England) I cannot avoid remarking, that it no doubt has a tendency to promote the great degree of health and flow of spirits I observed them possessed of, and readily accounts for many

wishing to remain, whose years of banishment have expired.[8]

Cooking in such cottages was over the open fire indoors, or outdoors in a skilling (a lean-to with a simple skillion roof). Houses were already hot enough in the summer, so a detached kitchen was a sensible and almost universal solution; it also protected the main building from the risk of fire.

The washhouse, or laundry, was sometimes a shed joined to the kitchen or house. As far away from the house as possible was the last and least palatable of the outbuildings, the privy.

Lime being unobtainable, many of the early brick buildings had clay for mortar, and sometimes this proved unstable in wet and windy weather. Wattle-and-daub cottages often suffered from termite attack, weakening the structure and threatening the health and safety of the occupants.

A storm was a serious event, as evidenced by this report in the *Sydney Gazette* of 1804:

The effects of the late heavy and incessant rains have left their usual traces among the cottage habitations, few of which have totally escaped visible injury. The unabating shower that fell on Wednesday night without a moment's interval from dark til several hours after daylight, few plastered panels could resist; and had the violence of the weather not somewhat abated, many slight buildings must certainly have been washed totally away . . .

The mode of building, however, receives the improvement it so much stood in need of, as permanency is now more generally consulted than it had hitherto been. Some months since a ludicrous, tho' indeed distressing circumstances occurred in the purchase of one of these airy buildings that perhaps in seniority came short of few. The bargain concluded, the Vendor removed his chattels and effects to make room for his successor; who being by the intervention of a couple of days' very bad weather prevented from immediate occupancy, upon the third proceeded to possession by entry; but had the unspeakable mortification to find that he had too long suspended his design, as the house had taken leave of the premises and left scarce a handful of rubbish in its place.[9]

Floods were one problem; fire was quite another. Most cottages had by that time some sort of fireplace, but many were of dubious construction. 'A friend to the Cottager' wrote in 1804:

I observe in passing to and fro the country, how industriously many are employed building comfortable cottage habitations, and much it is to be regretted that after all their labour and pains they are perpetually in danger of taking fire, owing to their chimnies being built with wattles. This mode of building chimnies may possibly be attributed to the want of a little regulation in the charges made for bricks, of which there are but few makers, and these, fearless of opposition, make such charges as upon enquiry must appear exorbitant.

Were the prices somewhat more reasonable, the use of bricks would become more general, and the makers eventually consider a reduction as advantageous to themselves as beneficial to the public; and the cottager's family might retire to rest without any apprehension of the danger to which the wooden chimney ever must expose them.[10]

The cost of glass was equally outrageous, prompting some emancipated felons to return to crime:

An extraordinary depredation was committed on the night of Tuesday last, at the untenanted house of Mr Mann ... the glazed sashes of which were every one carried off. Next day they were found by some children diverting themselves in the brush behind the latter, but in a state of improved transparency, as all the glass had been taken out, and the frames thus disposed of by the ingenious pillager, whose perhaps suspicious character suggested the apprehension of a search possibly taking place; in the event of which he very naturally inferred, that 'a bird in the bush was worth two in the hand'. In spite of cunning and precaution, however, suspicion perched upon a man whose general conduct had attracted a jealous eye, and much to the satisfaction of the neighbourhood the suspected bird of night retired to his cage.[11]

Meanwhile in Van Diemen's Land, far from the sophistication and urban chaos of Sydney, the trials of first settlement were being repeated. Huts were built in the same style as their northern counterparts, but with knowledge born of past experience improving the construction:

The huts were of most primitive construction being for the most part ... wattle-and-daub with a rush thatch ... Four corner posts were stuck in the ground, and upon these wall-plates were rested or nailed; further uprights were then added, and long rods of wattle from the bush were interwoven with the uprights, openings being left for door and windows. Mortar was then made of clay and loam, into which was mixed and beaten up wiry grass chopped up as a substitute for hair. The mortar was dabbed and plastered against the wattles outside and in, the roof covered in with flag-grass, a chimney built of stones and turf, a door and window added, the earthen floor levelled, and a coat of whitewash completed the cottage. In less than two months ... the huts were completed.[12]

On 1 January 1810, Lachlan Macquarie became governor of New South Wales. Macquarie was a humanitarian and a visionary with a love of orderly conduct — and orderly planning. He was shocked by the haphazard nature of development in the colony and set out to do what he could to create a planned environment by introducing building regulations. In a general order on 15 December 1810 he laid down that:

The dwelling houses are to be either made of brick or weatherboard, to have brick chimnies and shingled roofs and no dwelling-house is to be less than nine feet high — a plan of a dwelling house and offices will be left with each District Constable to which each settler must conform in the erecting of his building.

Macquarie also made land grants conditional on a minimum standard of building. The following general orders were issued in Hobart on 1 December 1811:

His Excellency the Governor, having observed

with much regret, since his arrival here, that the several Public and Private Buildings in Hobart Town have hitherto been erected in a very irregular manner and without any Plan whatever, has judged it expedient, and essentially necessary for the better appearance of the Town itself, and the accommodation of the Inhabitants, to frame and mark out a regular Plan of it for the future guidance and observance of all such Persons as may be permitted to reside and build in it . . .

No person in future is to presume to build a House of any description in Hobart Town without previously Submitting a Plan thereof to the Commandant, and receiving his Sanction for erecting the same. Such Persons as are able and willing to build Brick or Stone or weather boarded Houses, of two Stories high, forty feet long by 16 feet broad in the Clear, tiled or Shingled and properly Glazed,

will be entitled, on entering into security for erecting such a Building within two years, to receive a Town Allotment of 100 Feet in Front and 132 feet in depth, with 21 years Lease of the same from the Governor in Chief. Such Persons as are not able to build two Story Houses but are willing and able to erect Houses of one Story High, thirty six feet long by 14 feet broad in the clear, tiled or Shingled and properly Glazed, on entering into security to erect the same within two years, shall be entitled to receive a Fourteen years Lease from the Governor in Chief of a Town Allotment consisting of Sixty feet in front and 132 feet in depth.[13]

Even settlers in the country were affected by Macquarie's desire for quality, although their efforts may not have conformed to his rigid standards. Emigrant William Thornley, arriving in

Illustrated in 1806, G.P.R. Harris's cosy thatched home at Hobart Town, Van Diemen's Land, is essentially an English farm cottage transplanted 20 000 kilometres to a new and alien landscape.
NATIONAL LIBRARY OF AUSTRALIA

33

Mr Robinson's house at Hobart in the 1820s. Its Georgian lines have already been compromised to suit changing tastes by the addition of a mansard roof and an enclosed portico.
NATIONAL LIBRARY OF AUSTRALIA

Van Diemen's Land in 1817, describes a farmhouse near the town of New Norfolk:

I beheld before me a low building which I afterwards ascertained was built of the logs of the stringy-bark tree, split in half, and set on end. The building was about thirty feet long and white-washed. Its roof was composed of shingles, that is, of slips of wood about fifteen inches long, nine inches broad, and about half an inch thick. At one end of the house was a rough-looking piece of stone-work, formed of irregular pieces of stone procured near the spot, and forming the end wall and chimney. At one side was a garden, paled in with palings of the stringy-bark tree split into pales. I could see in the garden an aspect of the most luxuriant vegetation. In front of the house a small tree was left standing, and from one of the boughs of which was suspended a sheep newly killed.

We entered the habitation which consisted of one spacious apartment, opening into the air. At the end opposite the chimney a space was divided off into two small bedrooms. Opposite to the entrance of the house a door led to a skillion which served as a kitchen. In the middle of the principal apartment was a rough table of boards, on which was disposed sundry tin pannikins, a few plates, and some old knives and forks. A gigantic green bottle, containing rum, graced one corner of the table, and in the centre was set, as a place of honour, the pannikin of milk which had been obtained by the united efforts of the establishments within reach.[14]

On Thursday 28 February, Thornley took up his

land grant and began work on a cottage with the help of his foreman Crab and a small gang of assigned labourers:

I walked over my land, guessed, as well as I could, the extent of twelve hundred acres, and, after a good deal of examination of the parts about, settled on the spot for building our log-house. I thought the time might come when I should be able to erect a better house, so I marked a place for our temporary habitation close to the spot for the future building to form a part of the general plan. After this I set to work to help Crab and the men split logs for the hut. My wife said that she didn't like me to call it a hut, so I made a memo, to call it a cottage . . .

The next few days were spent in chopping, sawing, and splitting. Crab took it upon himself to select the timber and therefrom split the shingles. He wanted to know if I was going to build a town. He said it was a pity to take so much trouble about a thing which I may leave, perhaps, next day, but my thoughts were different.

On Friday 8 March 1817 we began to set up the walls of the cottage and eleven days later we had progressed as far as partly shingling the roof . . .

We finished the shingling, and now I was puzzled about the chimney which I had planned to be at one end. I went in search of some suitable stone, and I did not have far to look, for there were stones aplenty lying loose on the ground, but when I made to pick them up, I saw some monstrous black ants crawling about . . .

By the middle of April the cottage was completed, even to the stone chimney. For the mortar we had used some sandy loam and clay from the river-bed, and it seemed to make cement good enough for our purpose. The stone was easy to work, readily breaking into suitable shapes and handy sizes. The nights were now getting cold, but with a blazing fire in the new fire-place, the table in the middle of the room with Betsey's green cloth on it, and us seated on our logs of wood, we formed a cheerful party at supper.

I rose early one morning, according to my custom, and surveyed my new dwelling with particular satisfaction.

'No rent to pay for you,' said I, 'no taxes, that's pleasant; no poor rates, that's a comfort; and no one can give me notice to quit, and that's another comfort. And it's my own, thank God, and that's the greatest comfort of all.'[15]

In November Thornley gave the cottage the finishing touches:

I had long since plastered the cottage inside and out with sand and river clay, and now I gave the outside a coat of whitewash made from some whitish earth which my shepherd had found about six miles from the cottage. I now gave the inside a coat of wash made from the whiting and some of the red ochre which is abundant in some parts of the country. This produced something of a salmon colour, and as the plaster was smooth, the ochre gave it the appearance of stucco, and it looked very well and seemly.

We began to think something of ourselves, and would have assumed airs of importance, only there was no one near to show them to.[16]

In comparison with the majority of settlers, Thornley was a perfectionist. Another first-hand description of typical slab hut on the Hawkesbury River in the 1820s paints a rather more gloomy picture:

All these structures were composed of the then unvarying materials of Australian architecture in the interior — slabs or thin pieces split off by means of mauls and wedges from logs, the roof covered with forest box or stringy-bark, which was stripped from the living trees in sheets of about six feet long and from two to four feet wide, laid upon rafters composed of small sapling poles just as they came from being cut in the bush. The sheets of bark, having holes pierced through each in pairs, were then tied on the rafters with cords twisted of the inner rind of the kurrajong tree. The whole framing of the roof was secured as it was needed by wooden pins in order to save the expense of nails, which were then both too scarce

Government House, Windsor, was built around 1800 in a style typical of large Australian farmhouses. When this photograph was taken in the 1870s, the building was in some disrepair.
MITCHELL LIBRARY

and too dear to be used by the lower order of settlers.

Indeed, all kinds of ironwork were equally inaccessible, and instead of hinges to the doors or window shutters, those appurtenances were all made to revolve on wooden pivots in holes, bored a short distance into the corresponding parts of the frames.

Thus the materials of Mick's habitation were pretty much the same as those of the prisoners' huts on Emu Plains; but the chinks in the slab walls of the former were well stopped up with plaster made of cow dung and sand. A bark ceiling also was laid over the tie-beams which, while it prevented the dust from pouring down in such torrents through the interstices of the roof, also afforded a convenient loft for the storage of pumpkins and many other articles of domestic consumption. Besides these indications of comfort, the whole of the inside had been newly whitewashed — that is, *only* the Christmas before, though in the eleven months which had intervened the volumes of smoke which continually rolled through every cranny of the place had somewhat tarnished the virgin purity of its hue, converting it at length into a whity-brown yellow; yet even *that* colour was better than none.

As usual, the fireplace occupied nearly the whole of one end of the hut, and being composed entirely of wood, the danger of its igniting had been diminished by hard dried clods of clay built up about a couple of feet high round its interior and laid in a sort of mortar also composed of clay tempered with water to a semi-liquid consistency. On the sides of the ample fireplace were constructed rough seats for the winter nights, above which might be seen pieces of salted beef and pork, pigs' heads, bags of cabbage and pumpkin seeds, and a multitude of other articles which required to be kept dry, this being by courtesy considered the most secure part of the dwelling from the incursions of rain. There was no possibility of any leakage, *except* from the top, which was not *more* than two feet square, and left quite open in the fond hope of persuading or enticing the smoke to go out there instead of continually struggling for passage through the crevices of the bark roof or pouring out in volumes at the ever open doors and windows. But such was the perversity of this obstinate element that it too generally preferred any illicit vent to the legal one and very frequently asserted its supremacy in such a manner as effectually to drive the inmates out of doors altogether, for sheer lack of breath to continue the contest any longer. As this generally took place in very wet weather, when a fire could not be maintained out of doors, as was the usual summer custom, and besides, the chilliness rendering it acceptable in the

house for its warmth, it may be conceived that the piety of the inmates, at no time very conspicuous, was not vastly enhanced by their having to stand in the rain, perforce, in order to escape suffocation, until it pleased the vaporous enemy to allow them a short respite by retiring to the loft or any other part of the premises, *except the chimney of course*, which it appeared most of all places to shun.

The furniture was truly of a primitive cast. A number of tin pint pots and dishes, half a dozen three-legged cast-iron boilers of various sizes, a long-handled frying-pan, a few rough stools, mostly fixed on stumps sunk in the floor, two or three short round blocks of wood cut off trees with a cross-cut saw to serve as movable seats, and two stationary tables made of unplaned slabs, one fixed in the centre and the other on one side, completed the accommodation of the outer apartment.

When the doors of any of the sleeping-rooms admitted a view of their contents, it did not appear

that luxury was by any means the besetting sin of either Big Mick or his family. The sleeping-berths were all fixtures, made of slabs and sheets of bark, only the one belonging to the father and mother being furnished with any attempt at curtains, which for economy's sake were confined to the foot of the bed and one side. The berth being fixed in a corner, all was thus enclosed, partly by the slabs and partly by the curtain, which exactly answered the description given by Pope of those 'in the worst inn's worst room', being tied with tape and never meant to draw; instead of which, the blue striped shirting of which it was composed was secured back by loops and buttons which hung them partly aside and exposed to view a tattered patchwork quilt, apparently innocent of the washing-tub since its formation.

The effeminacy of sheets was unknown to any of the inmates. Though they obtained abundance of feathers, which, when plucked from the birds on

Half horizontal slab, half stone-and-shingle roofed, this early cottage at Newcastle, NSW, has a primitive wooden chimney unusual in a building with at least some walls of stone.

37

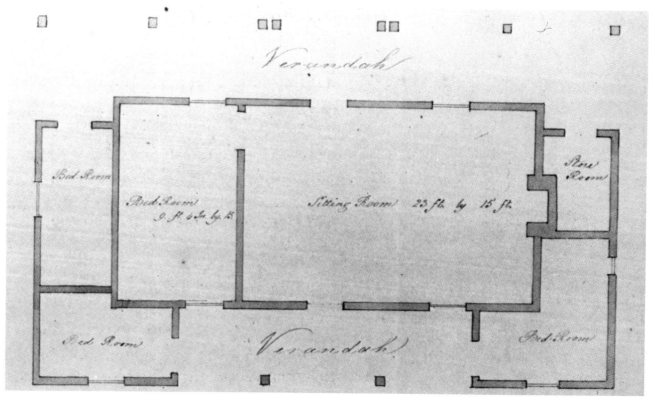

Glendon, designed and built by the Scott brothers. Georgian columns beneath a shingled roof join with a wide verandah to add harmony and elegance to what is really a very simple building. Its plan demonstrates how the verandah was used as a passageway between rooms. The kitchen and washhouse were separated from the main building to reduce the risk of fire.
MITCHELL LIBRARY

which they grew, were suffered to lie on the spot where they fell until dispersed by the winds, when they sailed about in all directions, a positive nuisance, yet each of the family slept on beds of chaff contained in rough ticks, many of which, being the worse for wear, suffered their contents to escape through their numberless orifices, when it littered the earthen floor. Being scattered thence into unknown corners, where brooms never penetrated, the rubbish proved fruitful nurseries of 'flaas', to the extreme annoyance of the good matron of the house, who strove in vain to abate it by repeated libations of water, until mud was by no means a scarce article, either within or without the domicile.[17]

Several steps up the social ladder from Big Mick's hut was the bungalow built by the English brothers Helenus and Robert Scott on their land-holding near Singleton in 1825. In a letter to his sister, Augusta Maria, Helenus included a floor plan, an elevation and the following brief description of the house they had christened Glendon: 'This is the plan of our cottage; the two centre rooms are a sitting and a bedroom which compose the body of the cottage; the rest are verandah rooms, three of which will make very good small bedrooms . . . the kitchen is a separate building . . . at the N.W. corner — How do you like the cottage?'[18]

Glendon's design utilised the verandah to provide access to rooms just as others had done, but soon country folk everywhere were discovering that in summer it was hard to find a more comfortable spot to relax; the verandah also protected the walls of the house from rain and weather, a factor that encouraged some settlers to experiment with new materials and construction techniques.

'Earth From the Site' 1820-1840

Resolved — That the mode of Building in Pisé, or rammed earth,
appearing to this Society to be both economical and expeditious, and from the Experience
of James Gordon, Esq., Vice-President of the Society, to be easily practised in this Colony;
the Society earnestly recommend its Adoption in Van Diemen's Land.
Information of the Means to be pursued will be readily afforded to any Person who
will address himself to the Society.

H.J. Emmett, Secretary

THIS NOTICE, INSERTED BY THE AGRICULTURAL SOciety on 10 May 1823, appeared on the front page of the *Hobart Town Gazette and Van Diemen's Land Advertiser*. Many took advantage of the Society's generous offer of information and soon substantial pisé buildings such as Wanstead Park near Campbell Town began to appear.

Some colonists, including William Thornley, were more wary. Having lost his first house (mentioned in the previous chapter) in a bushfire, he was in no hurry to lose another in a flood and thus sought the advice of his aptly named foreman:

It was on a bright frosty morning in the month of June 1825 that I summoned Crab to a cabinet council on the subject of our projected new house. I was inclined to try a new mode of building which had lately been introduced in the Colony, under the name of pisé building, the material for the walls being loam sieved free from stones and rammed hard. I did not want to build another house of wood, after having one go up in smoke ...

'Come, Crab,' said I. 'Give us your advice about a pisé house, as you have seen them and I have not. Will they do?'

'Do! Lord bless you! Never think of making a mud-pie and calling it a house. But why talk of a mud house when you have plenty of stone on your own land?'

'Yes,' said I, 'but stonemason's work is very expensive in this country.'

'Everything is expensive in this country,' said Crab, 'but you should have thought of that before you came to the miserable place.'[1]

Robert Gouger, a settler in the infant colony of South Australia, was more enthusiastic. In a letter home in 1837 Gouger pointed out that, apart from stone, pisé was the most durable and the cheapest mode of building. His letter contained a brief but helpful description of the method:

My own residence is thus built, and it is at once cool, substantial, and of a finished appearance. The process is simple, but to have justice done by the workmen, the constant eye of the master is required; with this care, a very excellent and cheap house can be erected. The walls are composed of earth (a fine friable loam is the best) rammed hard in a frame about six feet long by three feet high, and supported by moveable props on the walls. The walls can be of any thickness; and this should be proportioned to the height of the rooms and weight of roof intended. Spaces can be either left for the doors and windows, or they can be cut out afterwards; but if the latter mode is adopted, it should be done as soon as the work is completed, or the mass hardens, and the operation of cutting out is likely to injure the work. Should you go to the province without making yourself practically acquainted with the mode to be pursued, so many persons are there who do now understand it, that you will experience no difficulty. The cost of

Facing page
Colonel Light, founder of Adelaide, painted his 'View of proposed town of Adelaide' in about 1836. On the far right is the colony's wattle-and-daub Government House.
MITCHELL LIBRARY

41

Rammed earth utilising a sandy loam was probably the best known and, initially, the most widely used. Adobe, or mud brick, was another method that quickly became popular. These bricks were easily made from soils with a higher clay content: the earth was simply mixed with water and a little straw or grass (to prevent it cracking as it dried), moulded and left in the sun to dry.

This work was one of the many tasks undertaken by women. E.J. Hammond, describing the lives of pioneers in Perth, wrote: 'I have seen women making the clay brickbats, and I knew of one woman who made enough brickbats to build a five-roomed house.'[3]

A considerable advantage of mud bricks was that they could be used as soon as they were thoroughly dry; firing was unnecessary:

Above: photographed in the 1860s, a pisé house on the then outskirts of Adelaide has a small shingled porch which will one day become a verandah running the full length of the house. SLAPE FAMILY ALBUM

Right: this small pisé cottage near Richmond, Tasmania, is believed to have been built in 1833. A ducted fireplace and 45-centimetre-thick walls make it a snug home in a bitter southern winter. IAN HICKMAN

It will not always occur that the young beginner will have either the time or the money at his disposal for burning bricks — if he has, he is well off. Sun-dried bricks, if mixed with chopped straw, and carefully made, are an excellent substitute for the burned brick, and as they may be made very large, say, nine inches wide and eighteen-and-a-half inches long, they are very quickly laid. In Victoria there is, in general, a scarcity of lime: it can be always had in Melbourne though but seldom in the country. A mortar made of sandy clay or loam must, therefore, be substituted for it.[4]

building the walls is about 4s. 6d. a square yard of a foot thick: it will require plastering, which will be about 1s. 6d. a yard more. By means of these data, you will at once calculate the expense of the walls of the house you think you may require. If you want your house otherwise than a ground-floor, the walls of the lower part should be two feet thick, in which case, of course, the cost of working it will be enhanced.[2]

When all building materials had to be brought so far, it obviously made good sense to use earth from the site where possible. There were several techniques for this, all of great antiquity.

Wattle and daub — simple, quick and direct — continued to be used. It is possible to build, plaster and finish a small hut in a day, which explains its lasting popularity with immigrants in a hurry to house themselves and their families.

Although most of these huts were simply built in the traditional way, with an armature of wattles or branches plastered inside and out, a more substantial and stronger structure resulted if the clay was sandwiched between an outer and an inner skin of laths or split boards. This created a well-insulated house and eliminated the possibility of rain eroding the walls. Adelaide's first Government House was built in this style:

The only public-building which was intended to be of a permanent nature, is the government-hut. It is sometimes called 'Government-house', but I, who think the governor of South Australia ought to reside in a house capable of receiving and entertaining the colonists, and of impressing the passing visitor with an idea of gentlemanly style and English comfort, cannot dignify the place in which his Excellency resides, as a 'Government-house'. It is constructed of mud, put between laths, supported by uprights of native wood, and it is covered thickly with thatch. There are three rooms in it, with some little offices on one side, with a kitchen and servants' apartments detached. You will smile, when I tell you, that in the plan fire-places were forgotten, and that a single fireplace and chimney has now been put down close to the front-door; but recollect, that the architect was a sailor, and that

the workmen employed were the seamen of the Buffalo, who, thinking they could 'rig up a house', as well as a top-mast, would not allow any interference in their arrangements.[5]

Not all wattle-and-daub houses were slapdash affairs. In Western Australia the dynastic Bussell family, founders of the present city of Busselton, built in the 1830s a substantial two-storied homestead which they named Cattle Chosen in honour of a lost cow who had, after a sojourn in the bush, voluntarily returned to the fold.

In a letter written in January 1836, Fanny Bussell glowingly described the group of houses, set in a large garden, to her friend Capel Carter:

It is indeed a sweet place and improvements are daily springing up around us. The house we now occupy would strike at a distance as a comfortable

Angmering House at Enfield, SA, was begun around 1840 by John Ragless and gradually extended by a series of wings. Its vast thatched roof would have required some weeks to replace. STATE LIBRARY OF SA

43

Above: Victorian industry at its best: in one of the mid-nineteenth century's innumerable mining towns, M. Francis has set up shop before his wattle-and-daub house and smithy are finished.
MITCHELL LIBRARY

Right: when it was photographed in 1905, this charming wattle-and-daub cottage in the Adelaide Hills was already sixty years old. The outside walls are deteriorating through lack of maintenance.
STATE LIBRARY OF SA

The Bussell family in the grounds of their home Cattle Chosen at Busselton, WA, in 1867. In a letter written in 1836 Fanny Bussell had described the house on the right as 'most beautifully plastered so that not a crack is visible'.
BATTYE LIBRARY

substantial-looking mansion. It is white, and the four upper windows in the upper storey give it a cheerful and finished look, which perhaps it does not quite deserve.

As you approach it the garden, well fenced and productive in all English vegetables, would almost make you forget that you are in Australia. You would stop to admire Phoebe's cottage, first building after the barracks in the precincts of Cattle Chosen. John's house, near the garden, very comfortably fitted up as a bedroom for himself and Vernon, and ornamented with shelves containing his books, would almost make you in love with his little hermitage. By following the garden fence you approach the cottage shared between Lenox and Alfred. All these buildings have chimneys, and as winter is now approaching a bright fire not infrequently blazes on their hearths.

I have now brought you to our own house, which you gain by skirting the stock-yard bounded by a fence on two sides and by the river on the others. Our sitting-room is a well-sized and well-

proportioned room which we are gradually rendering comfortable and civilised. The walls of wattle and daub have been most beautifully plastered, so that not a crack is visible. The floor is of clay and the front door opens upon a pretty, cheerful pasture land, ornamented with some magnificent trees, but not heavily timbered, like Augusta. Our books are now arranged on shelves extending the whole length of the room. By the front door we have manufactured a species of couch, covered with your drugget, dear Capel.

The piano occupies its place under the window; our two sea-chests which Vernon has painted white, stand in a corner. Our noble chimney occupying nearly one side of the room gives promise of many a brilliant winter blaze. This is as yet our only finished room. The room upstairs forms a dormitory for all the females of the family.[6]

Sometimes wattle-and-daub walls were carefully and evenly plastered, incised to resemble

Tent, slab hut, pisé cottage ... then, as a badge of success, a grand brick or stone farmhouse. Wallcliffe House was built in 1865 for Alfred Bussell, at Margaret River, WA.
BATTYE LIBRARY

ashlar stonework, then whitewashed to produce a 'respectable finish', like the walls of the house built in Perth in the 1820s by the registrar-clerk of the Civil Court, Alfred Hawes Stone. Alpha Cottage was so named because it was the first building in St George's Terrace, one of the city's main streets. Stone's plan of the house and garden has some of the qualities of an early primitive painting, revealing much of the family's way of life and cultural background.

It seems that the building containing the bedrooms was constructed first, giving the family two rooms to live in while the house was extended to provide the dining room, office and front parlour. The kitchen was some distance from the house, to which it was linked by a covered walkway, and the servants' room, workshop, stable, store and 'open wash house' were all under the same roof. This arrangement ensured that the heat of the ovens in summer would not affect the living quarters, a concept that would continue to be employed, particularly by country people, for many years.

Any inconveniences — such as carrying hot dishes to the dining room — were borne largely by the servants, and devices to keep food hot, such as silver meat covers or containers that held hot water below the serving dishes, were frequently used. Although they had the simplicity and informality of cottages, houses like Cattle Chosen and Alpha Cottage often contained elegant furniture, china and the other refinements of 'civilised' life.

Not far from Alpha Cottage in St George's Terrace was Mona Cottage, one of the first prefabricated houses in Western Australia. Mona Cottage was made by John Manning, a London carpenter and builder who began by building a portable wooden house for his son to take to the Swan River. Quick to see the business potential of the idea, Manning developed a system of grooved posts between which doors, windows, or solid timber panels could be slotted. By 1830 he was directing his advertising to prospective migrants:

Gentlemen emigrating to the New Settlement,

A keen photographer, Alfred Hawes Stone chronicled almost every aspect of life at Alpha Cottage. Above his wife Maria (left) and a lady friend pose in 1863 on the new verandah, added in front of the parlour.
BATTYE LIBRARY

Progress continues along St George's Terrace. Alpha Cottage is about to be eclipsed by a new cottage whose milled framing timbers are stacked neatly, ready for the builders.
BATTYE LIBRARY

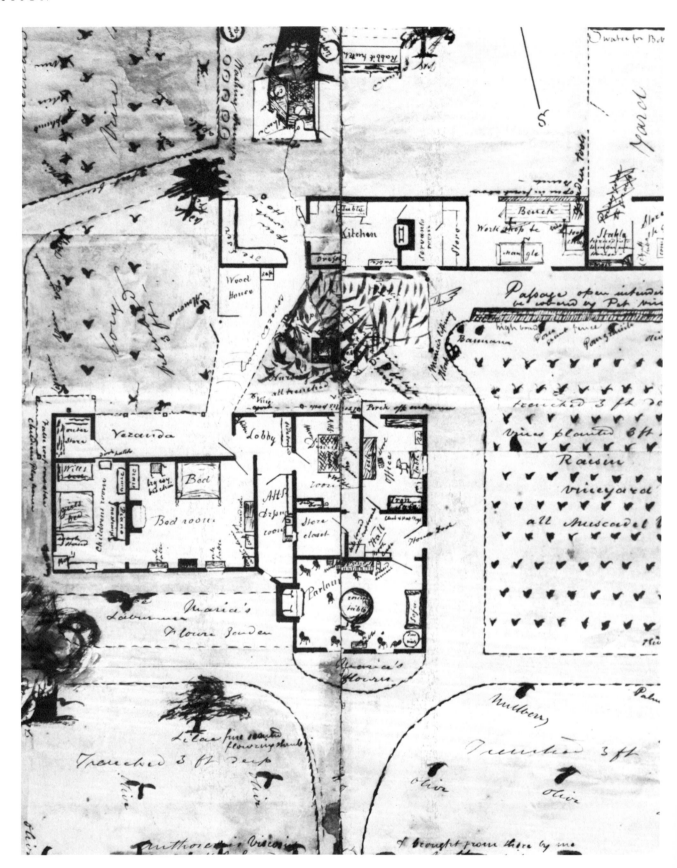

Alfred Hawes Stone
drew this plan of his
wattle-and-daub Perth
home, Alpha Cottage,
around 1839, carefully
delineating almost every
plant and piece of
furniture.
BATTYE LIBRARY

Above: pocket grandeur is an enduring feature of Australia's domestic architecture. Photographed in about 1860, G.J. Stone's home in St George's Terrace was no exception.
BATTYE LIBRARY

Left: not far along St George's Terrace from Alpha Cottage stood Mona Cottage, one of the first prefabricated houses to be erected in Western Australia. A more sophisticated version of the pioneer's slab hut, it relied on wooden panels set between grooved uprights.
BATTYE LIBRARY

H.W. Reveley's portrait, 'My house and garden in Western Australia, September 1833', testifies to the builder-engineer's diligence, from the water-powered mill (left) to his vegetables, ducks and hens.
NATIONAL LIBRARY OF AUSTRALIA

Swan River, on the Western Coast of Australia, will find a great advantage in having a comfortable Dwelling that can be erected in a few hours after landing, with windows, glazed doors, and locks, bolts, and the whole painted in a good and secure manner, carefully packed and delivered at the Docks, consisting of two, three, four, or more roomed Houses, made to any plan that may be proposed; likewise Houses of a cheaper description for labouring men, mechanics, &c. &c.

Manning's campaign was so successful that when South Australia was founded his houses were the most popular choice with new settlers. In addition to simple huts, he provided his wealthier clientele — including Governor Hindmarsh — with houses designed specifically for their requirements.

Robert Gouger advised that:

Of wooden-houses, those made by Manning of Holborn, are by far the best; nor are they too dear to be within the means of most colonists. Their great advantage consists in their portability, and their being very easily erected or removed. I took out a small room made by him, and some of my friends bought of him large houses. They have answered remarkably well, and by far surpass any other wooden houses in the colony. They are covered with a tarpaulin, and this is the best temporary covering you can have at first; as soon as you can, however, you will find it expedient to substitute for the tarpaulin the colonial roof of shingles. I took out blue slates, and my house is covered with them; but this expense is unnecessary, though for durability and appearance there is nothing to equal to them. The expense of a shingle roof is trifling.[7]

Early days of settlement anywhere were always chaotic, and to have an immediate shelter was a distinct advantage. Although carefully planned, the city of Adelaide took some time to develop a sense of order. One observer wrote in 1839:

At that time it resembled an extensive gypsy encampment. Not the semblance of a street existed on the land, although all the main streets had been duly laid out on the plan. It was in fact an extensive woodland, with here a solitary tent and there a cluster of erratic habitations. There were canvas tents, calico tents, tarpaulin tents, wurleys made of branches, log huts, packing case villas and a few veritable wooden huts.[8]

One of these huts was a temporary timber house brought out by George and Sarah Brunskill, who arrived in March 1839. Sarah wrote that accommodation was in very short supply:

We live in one half and our servants in the other. Fancy sleeping in a building with both ends open, only a piece of green baize hung at one end and nothing at the other. We are going to make a house worth living in and I do not mind the makeshifts when there is so much to look forward to.[9]

But there were compensations, too. Predating soap commercials and their obsessions by a century, Sarah went on to point out: 'The sun dries out washing as fast as we hang out, and it whitens more than a week's frost would in England. Had you seen my clothes, when we landed, you would have thought them spoilt, but they are as white as ever again.'[10]

The colour of their washing was the least of the problems facing the family of John Ridley, whose experience of portable dwellings left something to be desired:

My father, more fortunate than some of the pioneers, did not need to 'pitch his tent' in this literal fashion when he took possession of his Hindmarsh 'section'. He was glad enough to find on this property a small cottage of mud (pésé) in which to take shelter during the erection of a wooden house which he had brought from England in portions easily fitted together. At first, with a canvas cover for roof, the floor of hard clay seemed satisfactory enough, and my mother was glad to move from the hut to the larger rooms. Unfortunately they had not counted on rain. But the rain came, and it came down as it is still wont to do when it once begins. The canvas ceiling soon filled with water, and in due time the water made its way through with a steady drip that barely left room for thankfulness that it was not an unbroken shower. My mother liked to recall, with her quiet smile and twinkle of the eyes, how during that night she sat up in bed, gathering her two wee babies under the shelter of an umbrella. But the worst came when morning light disclosed the clay floor as a mud swamp.

It was, however, only a very short time before the house was comfortably finished and these and other mirth-provoking episodes left behind for ever.[11]

Lacking a similar sense of humour, other well-to-do settlers found it difficult to cope:

In addition to unsuitable accommodation the want of servants was felt more heavily still by many ladies in those early days, who, in feeble health and delicately nurtured, were compelled to perform the most laborious of domestic duties, such as cooking in the sun at a camp fire and doing the washing for their families.[12]

Had they read 'Practical Hints Previous to Emigration', these ladies would at least have arrived with the appropriate equipment, including:

Domestic ironmongery; all useful cooking utensils of the same kinds as are common in England: do not be tempted to bring out gim-cracks in the shape of portable kitchens, warranted to do every thing; they generally do nothing. Cast-iron three-legged pots are much used in out-of-doors cookery in these colonies: they should be provided with a bale and cover; and on first settling in the bush a triangle and rack to support the pot is found convenient. Frying-pans and gridirons for cooking in the open air upon wood-fires should have handles four feet long.[13]

A settler's first camp may have been primitive, but imagination was already transforming a tent and a bark-and-sapling shelter into a slab hut, then a warm and comfortable farmhouse.
LATROBE LIBRARY

Wrestling with metre-long frying-pan handles must have been extremely difficult; flies also posed a problem:

The large meat-fly of Australia, be it known to you, instead of depositing the germ of maggots, deposits them actually living; in order to preserve meat therefore, hot, cold, or uncooked for a single day, go to a wire-worker's and purchase some wire gauze dish covers, and some pieces of strong but close wire-work, sufficiently large for the manufacture of a commodious safe.[14]

Of all the South Australian colonists the best organised was a large group of Germans who, like many Lutherans at that time, were fleeing from religious persecution in Prussia. These were mainly small landholders, farmers and artisans who, on arrival, formed into communities at Klemzig, Hahndorf and Lobethal, and later still moved into the Barossa Valley to found South Australia's wine industry.

Once the question of land tenure was resolved they wasted no time. Trees were felled, timber sawn and roughly dressed, clay prepared and rushes gathered for houses constructed after the style of the homes they had left behind. The *Southern Australian* of 1 May 1839 reports of Klemzig, today a suburb of Adelaide:

Four or five months only have elapsed since the hand of man began there to efface the features of the wilderness, yet nearly thirty houses have been erected, and good and spacious houses some of them are. All are neat, clean, and comfortable.

52

They are mostly built of pisé, or of unburnt bricks, which have been hardened by the sun. The more humble cottages consist of brushwood and thatch.

Another traveller observed dryly:

Four miles from [Mt Barker] is Hahndorf, a village essentially German in name and nature. On the way we observed a great many thriving potato crops, and cornfields that seemed to have yielded good harvests ... On each side of the road were cottages of the Germans, with their particular thatches, which looked ponderous and substantial ... The houses are very various, of stone, wood, pisé and a combination of all; but there are some great though rather dull-looking structures, with upper floors. The inhabitants are nearly 500, chiefly Germans — industrous, good-humoured, obliging,

and in many cases, intelligent.[15]

Many of the early houses of Hahndorf and nearby Paechtown were built using a traditional building technique from central Europe known as *fachwerk. Fachwerk*, or half-timbered construction, is similar to modern steel framing in that all the weight and stress is taken by horizontal and vertical members, assisted by diagonal braces. The gaps between these were filled in with wattle and daub and, later, brickwork.

The clay soils around Adelaide are well known for their instability, which has resulted in considerable damage to buildings over the years, and some observers noticed shrewdly that the half-timbered houses were more than simply picturesque. E.H. Hallack wrote in 1892:

A shotgun-carrying settler from Germany, his wife, and their eleven children pose proudly outside their well-constructed slab hut near Hahndorf, SA.
STATE LIBRARY OF SA

53

Above: German builders at Hahndorf, SA, soon became skilled in the use of local materials, modifying traditional infill or *fachwerk* designs to houses suited to the Australian climate.
STATE PROMOTION UNIT, SA

Right: this thatched cottage built by German settlers in the Barossa Valley, SA, is wholly European in its design, materials and philosophy.
STATE LIBRARY OF SA

the houses and their construction commend themselves as useful object lessons to builders on clayey or Biscay cracking soils. One of the oldest was built in 1840 on the Swiss or chalet lines of architecture, as are also many others here and in Friedrichstadt. Thatch for roofing, with brick walls intersected with gum-framing V-shaped, horizontal, and other shaped walled lacings, they score anything but cracks, the wooden lacements or bracings preventing the possibility of such. These 'German ideas' of building are well worthy of imitation and adaptation in many other localities. [16]

Because South Australian homebuilders were more intent on conforming to other, less practical, traditions and fashions imported from Britain, the value of the 'German ideas' unfortunately went largely unnoticed.

Another original building concept to appear in South Australia — that of building underground — was to have more important implications for future housing. In 1845, the South Australian Mining Association engaged ten miners from Cornwall to begin mining for copper at the Burra Burra Mine. They struck a bonanza and before long their numbers grew to 2000 plus. The company offered accommodation in overpriced small cottages and, rather than pay rent, most miners preferred to build their own shelters. One newspaper reported:

Upon arrival at the town the miner's first job was to dig himself a home — and who better than a miner to do this? Passage ways connected each of the three or four rooms of the dugout and sleeping recesses were dug into the walls. Along the front of the home there was a shingled verandah with windows. Inside the rooms were white washed, or papered. [17]

The dugouts were simply mined into the soft alluvial clay of the high banks of Burra Creek, and on the whole seemed to function quite well, according to this contemporary description:

This tiny two-roomed hut, with a shingle roof and a neatly plastered chimney, was built in 1845 next to the Lutheran parsonage at Lobethal, SA, as living quarters for students.
STATE LIBRARY OF SA

55

Above: William Anderson Cawthorne illustrated the underground homes of the miners at Burra Creek in 1851, for his 'Views of South Australia'. Note the chimneys that project above the houses.
MITCHELL LIBRARY

Right: rain and baking heat have already begun to erode the entrance to the Tonkin family's excavated cliff dwelling at Weston Flat Village, SA.
STATE LIBRARY OF SA

One of the most singular features however is the subterranean habitations of 'The Creek'. For a distance of more than 2 miles, the banks of a ravine are perforated with vaulted chambers, in which a populous community are living in apparent health and comfort. From above, these dwellings present a squalid but exceedingly diversified and picturesque appearance. Some are quite cottage like in their exterior, having stone fronts, well proportioned doors and windows, with verandah and fences guarding the approach. In those cases, the earth is cut away so as to give a perpendicular front and that secures a sort of terrace before the door; but in a great many instances there is a narrow horizontal cut, running sufficient far into the bank to gain a height for, and an approach to a door; a similar cut of smaller dimensions opens the way to a window and the remainder of the house is a perforation in the bank continued from these apertures.[18]

Life underground also had its lighter side:

Most of them were nicely furnished and all kept scrupulously clean and sweet by frequent white washings. Light was admitted by a window on each side of the door. Of course there could be only one entrance, the 'house' having neither back nor sides. A hole from the fireplace to the surface carried off the smoke; but as the road from the township to the mine passed over these dwellings, it was usual to place over these holes a cask with the ends knocked out, so as to prevent nocturnal travellers from falling into the kitchen below. Practical jokers, however, would sometimes remove these protections; and then the family at supper would probably be startled by the hurried and undignified entrance of an unbidden guest, whose language would often be more scriptural than religious. Sammy W. used to declare that he owed the possession of the best little wife in the world to one of those primitive chimneys.[19]

In February 1851 however, a nocturnal flash flood occurred, with the result that 'the tenants were unceremoniously expelled from their habitable grottoes'; a second flood sealed the fate of the settlement.

In June the mine owners declared the creek banks out of bounds, leaving many with nowhere to live. By coincidence news arrived by stagecoach that gold was being found in abundance in the east, and many miners left to try their luck in the new State of Victoria.

A smiling Son (or Daughter) of Australia poses for the family album against an incomplete wattle-and-daub wall.
BATTYE LIBRARY

'Father Tried to Improve it' 1840-1860

I must say that a worse regulated, worse governed, worse drained, worse lighted, worse watered town of note is not on the face of the globe; and that a population more thoroughly disposed, in every grade to cheating and robbery, open and covert, does not exist; that in no other place does immorality stalk abroad so unblushingly and so unchecked; that in no other place does mammon rule so triumphant; that in no other place is the public money so wantonly squandered without giving the slightest protection to life or property; that in no other place are the administrative functions of Government so inefficiently managed; that, in a word, nowhere in the southern hemisphere does chaos reign so triumphant as in Melbourne.

SO WROTE A CORRESPONDENT FOR THE SYDNEY *Morning Herald*, on 4 November 1852. Despite the disdain with which Sydneysiders have always regarded their southern sister city, it would appear that the portrait was not greatly distorted.

The arrival in the early 1850s of thousands of miners from all over the world, on their way to the gold diggings at Bendigo and Ballarat, resulted in a surge of unparalleled development, changing the character of Melbourne almost overnight. In a letter written at that time Antoine Fauchery expressed his surprise that:

Whereas I had expected to find wooden houses, huts even, hastily erected and scattered among the trees, I found houses of one or two storeys, solidly built, aligned as straight as a die, forming streets a kilometre long, very straight, very wide, perfectly macadamised, and in these streets black coats, collars, silk dresses, heeled boots, everything just as in Europe, everything including even barrel-organs.[1]

In the space of only seventeen years Melbourne had grown from an illegal settlement of weatherboard shanties and turf hovels. After its existence was officially recognised in 1835, surveyors Russell and Hoddle produced a plan based on a simple geometric grid with wide main streets, and people began building in earnest. Bricks were burned in wood-fired kilns down by the Yarra and a few

kilometres away suitable building stone was discovered in the form of a hard, dark grey basalt. This 'bluestone' was to become a distinguishing feature of Melbourne's architecture.

The atmosphere of peace and tranquillity evident in drawings of the city in the 1840s was shattered forever by the golden hordes. One of these, William Westall, was appalled by 'the scenes of riotous, drunken debauchery of Melbourne' and decided to look for quieter lodgings in the vicinity of the canvas city of Emerald Hill. He paints an amusing picture of the sort of houses money-hungry developers were building at the time:

close by there was a little street of weatherboard houses — the first erected there — and that probably they were not all let, as they were not all thoroughly finished. From the character of the neighbourhood I was desirous of securing a temporary resting-place in it, so I hurried across to the new buildings, where I was fortunate enough to find the landlord, and closed, without cavil, for one of the tenements, at the current rate of £4 per week, or £1 per room, such as they were. These houses, greedily snapped up at a rent equivalent to £208 per annum, were wretched hovels, roofed with rough shingles, which, although they led off the rain, allowed the wind and light to stream in through their interstices. The same description will suit the sides, on which the boards only overlapped enough to carry down the drip, though it frequently bubbled up in high winds, finding its way into the interior. The partitions were simply constructed of sized long-cloth, which admitted the convenience of conversing with your neighbour without the trouble of leaving your own apartment. The arrangement, however, admitted of this indelicate drawback, that if your candle at bedtime happened to be extinguished first, you might probably be startled by the shadowy phantom of Mrs or Miss A B C, next door, in her night-dress preparing for the stretcher. The floors, whether intentionally or not I can't say, were laid somewhat on the hencoop principle, so that all garbage or offal might fall through. I know that some of our knives, forks, and I think a blacking-brush, disappeared through these slender slits, which also admitted such copious currents of wind, that a long-six stearine rarely saw out our evening's repast. In fact, taking them for all and all, it would be considered at home cruelty to animals to use them as dog-kennels, and it would certainly vitiate a policy to force a person whose life you had insured to sleep in one of them for a single night. However, we were as proud and happy as possible in having even a shed in the colony that we could call our own.[2]

These 'sheds' were not confined to Emerald Hill:

Prahran, on the south of the town, has become a large village, at a distance of a mile and a half, and itself stretching as much further. St Kilda, three or four miles off, has grown equally. It is true the greater proportion of these houses are of one story, and are built of wood, — erections evidently not intended for eternity, nor for the encounter of any tolerable hurricane.[3]

The demand for any sort of accommodation was overwhelming. New portable houses of iron began to arrive from England and found a ready market. These were much lighter, cheaper and more compact to transport than the wooden prefabricated houses of a decade earlier, but the uninsulated corrugated iron roof and walls were often lined only with canvas, a fact many of their purchasers would later regret.

William Howitt wrote prophetically: 'These houses seem to have a vast demand, because they are rapidly put together; but they should send out iron constitutions with them, for the people who are doomed to inhabit them; for they will be very cold in winter, and in summer will just roast their tenants alive. They will prove admirable houses —for the doctors.'[4]

Facts and Figures, a whimsical little journal edited by one William Henry Archer, reported that during 1853: 'there were upwards of 4,000 additional buildings erected in Melbourne city alone; while in the suburbs, canvas and slab, and wattle and daub sprung up with mushroom rapidity, and a rank tropical growth.'[5]

It was a seller's market and the new breed of real estate agents, among them William Westall, waxed as lyrical as ever. In 1857 Westall offered, 'only five minutes' ride by railway from Melbourne':

a most neat and substantial cottage standing in the centre of its own grounds [containing] four convenient-sized rooms, with lobby. A verandah five feet in width surrounds the entire cottage, upon which the vine and numerous other creepers twine in graceful luxuriance, while a parterre of beautiful flowers fills up the foreground. A detached kitchen, servant's bed-room, and scullery complete the domestic offices; also a fowl-house and aviary, with sufficient unoccupied land on which to erect a coach-house and stable. The back windows of the cottage command extensive views of the Bush, and the plume-boarded beach lying between St Kilda and Brighton, while that bold promontory, the Red Bluff, Pic-Nic Point, with Mount Eliza in the distance, charm the scene.

The bay and harbour of Port Phillip, bearing on their waters the stately ships of many climes, bringing the world's merchandise to this El Dorado of ours, give new and charming features to the scene. The arrangements of this 'Gem of Emerald' are so complete, that it must be the fault of the occupier if comfort, peace, and happiness in their

M'LEAN BROS. AND RIGG, MELBOURNE.

PORTABLE IRON HOUSES.

These Houses are suitable for Squatters, Farmers, Selectors, Diggers, and others. They are simple of construction, **are *easily erected without skilled labour*,** and can be taken down again in a very short time.

They are complete in every respect, with doors, windows, locks, sash fasteners, and everything necessary for their erection. We recommend them especially to Squatters, Selectors, and Diggers, on account of the simplicity of their construction, their suitability to the requirements of the climate of these colonies, and their portability —being forwarded in packages of convenient dimensions. We have them with one, two, three, or four rooms.

PRICES.

			Without Flooring and Lining.		With Flooring and Lining.
One-roomed House	...	...	£16 0 0	...	£21 0 0
			(Forming a complete building.)		
Two-roomed „	...	...	£25 0 0	...	£35 0 0
Three-roomed „	...	...	£36 0 0	...	£52 0 0
Four-roomed „	...	...	£52 10 0	...	£70 0 0

Above: a view of Melbourne in 1841, looking across Collins and Swanston streets to the Yarra River and Hobson's Bay in the distance. The township has grown considerably in just one year.
NATIONAL LIBRARY OF AUSTRALIA

Left: this neat mid-nineteenth century prefabricated house, with an iron frame and corrugated iron cladding, had wooden window frames and was lined with tongue-and-groove boards.
JOHN ARCHER

61

Above: with walls of milled weatherboard and a formal row of wooden columns, Greenwood Station homestead, on the Richmond River, has a central hallway opening to the main rooms of the house.
J.W. LINDT, NATIONAL LIBRARY OF AUSTRALIA

Right: using the verandah as a covered passageway between rooms reduced the number of walls (and therefore the amount of construction work) in a farmhouse of the 1840s.

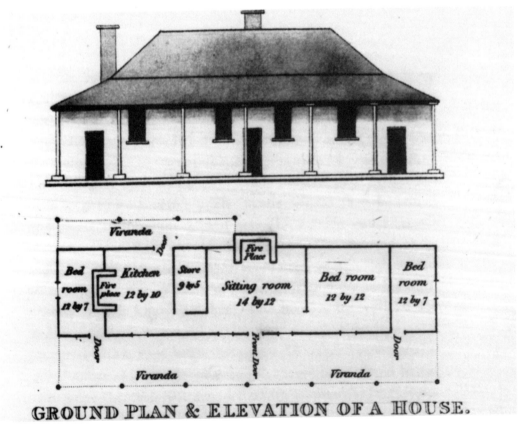

GROUND PLAN & ELEVATION OF A HOUSE.

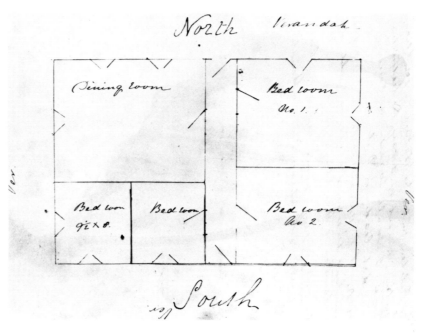

widest sense do not reign throughout the entire establishment.[6]

Five minutes' ride in the other direction lay the Jolimont house of Charles Perry, Anglican Bishop of Melbourne. His wife, Frances Perry, was one of many pioneer women whose letters, journals and sketchbooks have provided historians with sensitively detailed descriptions of their houses. When the Perry's house was being built in 1848, she wrote:

Our house that is to be contains two sitting-rooms, opening into one another with folding-doors, and three bedrooms — all on the same floor, as is the case with every house here . . . Then there is a small store-room, and at about five yards' distance is a small kitchen, with two closets in it, in which servants have hitherto slept — a coach-house, and stables for two horses. This is the whole of the premises. The flower-garden is of a moderate size, and there is a small kitchen-garden beyond; and beyond that the Government paddock. Before we go in, C is going to build two servants' rooms, attached to the kitchen; and join the kitchen to the house, by some kind of covered way. There is a verandah round three sides and a half of the house, and altogether it looks very pretty.[7]

Marian Cotton married Charles Ryan at the age of eighteen and set off with her groom on horseback for their honeymoon at Killeen Station, Mount Macedon. At the age of eighty she recalled:

Our old cottage at Killeen was built of pisa [sic] nearly sixty years ago now, and when I went to see it last year it was as strong and good as ever and so beautifully cool as the walls are two foot thick. To make pisa there is first a lattice work of wood, two feet in depth; the interior is filled with clay or earth and chopped straw and is rammed down very hard, then cemented all over outside, at least I suppose it is a sort of cement. It lasts for ever, far better than brick or stone, is beautifully cool and looks much better than anything else, no leakage anywhere. Killeen is the loveliest bush house I have ever seen. The verandah in front is twelve feet wide and in our time had chairs, tables and couches on it. In front hung a curtain of creepers and asparagus fern; there were long pergolas covered with vines and magnificent grapes. A hollow tree outside was made into a place for butter, milk, etc.: it was kept wet and the contents were always icy cold. The inside furniture of Killeen was made on the place and was quite original as we had a carpenter who was very artistic. It is mostly still there.[8]

Little more than a box for eating and sleeping, a Queensland settler's simple farmhouse of the 1860s is seen here in plan, and under construction. The steeply pitched roof — typical of the time and region — to some degree aided ventilation and cooling.
JOHN OXLEY LIBRARY

Deep in the cool damp forests of the Victorian Alps, an 1870s settler braves chills, rheumatism and leeches in a low hut made of tree-fern logs, with a canvas ceiling and a roof of stringybark.
LATROBE LIBRARY

A celebrity of the day, Mrs Charles Meredith, whose published works included *Notes and Sketches in New South Wales*, described in her book *My Home in Tasmania* how she and her husband had trouble reaching agreement over the design of their home near Riversdale. Similar difficulties are still experienced by couples today.

I made innumerable plans, each seeming in its turn perfectly unexceptionable, until my husband, with his awful precision of compasses and calculation of 'ways and means' ranged in array against me, proved one after another their impracticability. At last a partnership plan was concocted, to our mutual satisfaction, combining comfort and economy with a sufficient regard for appearance; and materials requisite for its completion were carefully calculated and ordered ...

The walls of our cottage were to be built of the common 'iron-stone' of the country, quarried from the bank where it was to stand, the cleavage of which very conveniently separates it into flat slabs of all sizes and thicknesses, suitable for rough stone buildings; and, when well-fitted and cemented together, and neatly faced with cut free-stone at all the corners, door and window cases, &c., it makes a most substantial fabric. Our outer walls were twenty inches thick, and the inner ones eighteen.[9]

By the end of August 1842 the cottage's construction had advanced to the point that it could be occupied:

and, without waiting for anything further, we began the welcome business of removal thither.

Never, perhaps, did the unpleasant process of changing one's house appear so delightful. The very carts and drays as they started off, loaded with the heterogeneous contents of our abode, had, in my eyes, quite a cheerful and jaunty air, as they went nodding along; and the promiscuous arrangement of chair and table legs looked as if scarcely restrained from a dance on the spot. My piano carefully replaced in its English case, and laid upon a dray well padded with bags full of straw, and drawn by six oxen, moved away with a grave and solemn demeanour, as if conscious how important a part it played in the procession, and would probably be much scandalised at the riotous and unmusical conduct of certain small pigs, who, with their portly maternal parent, occupied another vehicle in the train.

On the following morning, after breakfast, our horse-cart came to the door, and received its precious freight, consisting of the children, the mamma, the nurse, and the cat, the latter safely tied up in a bag, greatly to dear little George's amusement and mystification. Portfolios, desks, workboxes, books, toys, and such 'small deer', completed the load, and so we arrived at last at our new home. How busy everybody immediately became, what sounds of brooms and scrubbing-brushes, of mops and pails; what hammering and unpacking went noisily on, may well be imagined; but so merrily and rapidly went on the work, that even on the first night we were tolerably snug, and in another day or two were truly 'at home'.

Our walls were still damp, from their own great thickness, and the fresh plaster, one coat only of which we waited to have put on before removing, purposing to finish the interior in summer. Certainly the scores and crossing of the plasterer's trowel were not ornamental, and the dark colour of the walls might seem somewhat gloomy; but as soon as they dried sufficiently, I had a remedy at hand for all their unsightliness; I hung up the old pictures once-again, and heartily welcomed them to, as I then believed, their last Australian home.[10]

The Merediths built another, similar home at

Port Sorell and, like many colonial cottages, it was eventually modified and extended as time and circumstances permitted:

A spacious verandah, erected this summer along the front of the house, is the most important and essential addition of all; in this country, a good veranda is like an extra sitting-room; and, as an airy play-place for children on a warm or rainy day, is invaluable. We hope that some of our numerous families of swallows will take, or rather make, apartments in it next summer ... Our verandah also forms my only substitute for a greenhouse, and in this climate such partial shelter is sufficient for the cultivation of most plants which must be wholly protected during an English winter.[11]

A verandah was also an integral part of the slab cottage built in the New England district of New South Wales by Matthew Marsh for his bride Elizabeth, who wrote to her sister, Maria, in 1844:

The present cottage, or as they are more properly termed here, huts, is considered the most comfortable of all the squatters' places. It consists of a small passage about four feet wide with a door at each end; one door leading up to the verandah, the other being the main entrance and way from the kitchen, which is another hut about five yards distant. On the other side of the passage is our bedroom with a skillion leading out of it used as Matt's dressing room and on the other side of the passage are two similar rooms, one the sitting room and the other Mr Perkins' bedroom (Mr Perkins is the Superintendent). On each end of the verandah are two little rooms about seven feet long and six feet wide, one used as a spare bedroom and the other on my side of the house as a room for Millicent to work in, or for my use as maybe, but as there are but three chairs about the place, the other being stools, I find my bedroom when I want to lie down the most comfortable place — our bedroom looks really quite comfortable, for you do not as in the sitting room see daylight through the roof as there is a ceiling of canvas; but the sitting room is only

Above: Woodcutters Frank Williams and Bill Kidd pose with the tools of their trade (and their pipes) displayed on a pile of expertly hewn timber destined for railway sleepers.

Right: a magnificent Tasmanian gum is converted into fence palings to satisfy suburban dreams. The tree was sawn to length then cut into billets, which were then split with a froe or paling knife.
STATE LIBRARY OF TASMANIA

"SPLITTING SLABS"

canvas around the sides. It could be altered, but for summer use I think it better as it is. The whole hut is of wood, long pieces put upright but not exactly meeting, so that if there were no canvas around the inside it would be airy enough ...

Matt led me to expect a much worse residence, but I find nothing but what I can easily well put up with until the new house is finished ... We have fixed on a site for the new house and the timber is waiting, but we mean to have a good deal of stone about it to make the rooms more private, as through the wooden walls every sound can be heard all over the house.[12]

By far the most popular and readily available building materials of the time were hand-split palings, slabs, shingles and bark, and since they

could often all be obtained from the same tree there was little waste. After the tree was felled the bark, if useable, was removed in large sheets and put to one side. Then the timber was cut into appropriate lengths with a crosscut saw. Slabs were split from these, using wedges driven in with a heavy mallet. The billet was split in half, then halved again until slabs of the right thickness — generally about 70 millimetres — resulted.

These could then be dressed on their inside faces with a drawknife — a long curved blade with a handle at each end, used for smoothing and shaping rough timber. The drawknife was also used for dressing palings split from billets with a paling knife. Palings were usually about 15 millimetres thick and about 1.5 metres long, while the length of slabs depended on the type of construction used.

Splitting slabs on the Tweed River, NSW — a picnic occasion which combined hard work with the enjoyment of seeing the creation of materials for the family's new house.
JOHN OXLEY LIBRARY

67

Winter quarters for Maloga's 'station blacks', here receiving a visit from a Bible-carrying Victorian miss, were simple huts of horizontal slabs, with much-patched bark roofs.
NSW HISTORICAL PHOTOGRAPH RESOURCE CENTRE

Slab builders were divided into two schools of thought — the vertical and the horizontal. Vertical slab huts had large squared plates top and bottom, which were grooved so that the chamfered slabs could be slipped into place.

The horizontal style was the most popular. Grooved corner and intermediate posts were simply set in the ground and the slabs were inserted from above, one on top of another.

Whichever method was used, shrinkage caused gaps to appear between the slabs. One pioneer housewife, Georgiana McCrae, saw this as a new art form:

Our house is built of gum-tree slabs supported, horizontally, by grooved corner-posts, and the same artifice (used again) for windows and doors. The biggest room has been furnished with a table and chairs, but no pictures — long lines of actual landscape appearing at interstices between the planks instead! [13]

There were some health fanatics who saw this as a positive advantage:

There is seldom, however, in any hut a want of light, as the shrinking of the slabs causes innumerable openings in the walls all round and round, and light as well as fresh air are poured in as freely and bountifully as into a bird's cage in the open air. [14]

In winter, however, this airiness was less than ideal, and in practice it was common to plug the

cracks between the slabs with clay, and then to plaster the inside with white pipe clay, or to line it with boards or material. *The Australian Enquirer* pointed out in 1865 that:

The most effective lining for a slab hut is cretonne or chintz, fastened to the walls with small brass headed nails. Many of the rooms, even though built of sawn stuff, would be improved by a pretty lining. One room I saw done was most effective, having the appearance of a padded room; round the top the cretonne was gathered on to a hoop held up in some invisible way.[15]

But while the fabric lining presented a finished appearance, frogs and other wildlife often found a home behind it:

Centipedes used to live, too, between the canvas and the slab wall, where they would in their perambulations make eerie scratchings, and many a long hour have I been awake in cold horror, listening to the sound of the hundred feet on their travels, and getting as near to the outer side of the bed as was possible.

For in the bush we slept mostly on bunks made of sawn saplings nailed against the slabs.[16]

The bark hut which was the usual first house for settlers was built with material from their own selection. Bark-collecting also killed trees, the first step in 'improving' the land for farming.

69

Another feature of the typical slab hut was its enormous fireplace, which often occupied the whole of one end of a room. Sometimes these had been added as afterthoughts — cooking in the rain was no fun:

Our cooking was done in the open until my father took the liberty of cutting an opening in the wooden wall and building an outside chimney and fireplace of turf. On top of the chimney a sort of funnel of bark was erected to create a better draught and so we were able to indulge in the luxury of a warm fire. Our roof was none of the best, but mother was equal to the occasion, when the leaky places admitted the rain, by placing tin plates and dishes in position on the bed to catch the rain.[17]

The exterior of the fireplace was often clad with slabs or bark, like the rest of the hut, but lined inside with stone to prevent the walls catching fire. John Everett describes his hut as being 20 feet by 12 feet (6 metres by 3.5 metres) in size:

The fireplace at one end being very large like a farm house in England. The inside of the chimney to a height of about 3 feet is lined with rough stones, the centre one on top row being a picked one of triangular shape, which gives a finish to it. The remainder of the chimney is rough slabs. From the centre of the beam or pole which runs across the chimney is an iron hook to hang the kettle on; around the inside are a few cooking utensils. A slab forms a mantelpiece, and in a line with it on each side are two small book shelves.[18]

Simon McDonald recalled a similar style in his family home at Creswick, Victoria:

they built a mud-chimney with mud and stones, Dad and my uncle Jack. It would be about five feet wide at the bottom, and they used to put great billets of wood in, and on the winter's nights I'd stand on the hobs like and it was so big I'd really be standing in the chimney. My mother baked scones in the camp oven, and everything was cooked in the big iron pots those days. They scrubbed them and washed them; they had everything perfectly clean, and nobody was sick, or you might have been sick once in a year.[19]

Being sick once a year was a minor hazard compared with the threat of incineration. Because the

Above: a mid-Victorian patriarch and his obedient family pose outside their house of hand-split shingles and slabs near Port Pirie, SA. Note the chimney, also of hand-split wooden billets.
STATE LIBRARY OF SA

Facing page
A quartet of shy bush children in their Sunday best face the photographer outside their slab-sided, thatch-roofed cottage. New technology has arrived in the form of a fireproof metal chimney.
NATIONAL LIBRARY OF AUSTRALIA

Above: neat centrepiece of a tidy and well-organised farm, this slab cottage has a spacious verandah and a high ceiling for plenty of ventilation, both well suited to its subtropical location

Right: a farm building was simpler to construct than a house, if only because its timbers were not trimmed as neatly. The horizontal slabs used in this barn are simply posts trimmed at each end.
BATTYE LIBRARY

art of chimney building was not well understood by many bush carpenters, some chimneys — especially those built of split palings —were only lightly attached to the house so that, in the likely event of the chimney's bursting into flames, it could be demolished quickly.

George Easton, a Tasmanian settler with a rather unstable father, records that their chimney was constantly catching alight at the top:

father tried to improve it but made it smoke abominably, so we sat night after night with the smoke hanging within three feet of the floor and the rain pouring through the smoke all over the roof into tins and buckets. We would be forced to open the door to let the smoke out and then the cold air would flow in and we would freeze ...

As soon as my father could get away he went off to Sydney saying he was going where he could get

dry, and I pulled the fancy top off the chimney and got rid of the smoke nuisance.[20]

The floors in huts like this were usually of earth. The recipe for their construction was simple enough:

The old hands told me how to build a clean dirt floor:
Beat it hard with spades and tread of feet,
Then soak with green cow dung and sweep again.
Now sprinkle water, fire, and clear creek sand,
And sometimes strew with cool green leaves;
Sprinkle and sweep it twice a day
Until, clean and sweet and hard,
It gleams, black, polished like a board.[21]

According to the diary of West Australian, George Fletcher Moore, this was something that could wait for a rainy day. On one such he reported: 'Johnny mended his shoes; James made a mud floor

The bitter winters and chilly mornings of the mountainous Monaro district in southern New South Wales inspired the construction of massive fireplaces capable of warming even a draughty slab hut.
NATIONAL LIBRARY OF AUSTRALIA

73

Above: fireplaces like this, photographed in a settler's hut at Briagolong, Vic, were often large enough to accommodate several people as well as a cheery cooking fire on a chill winter's night.

A miner's whitewashed wattle-and-daub cottage at the Hill End, NSW, goldfields shows the arrangement of pegged and greenhide-secured 'riders' to keep the stringybark roof in place.
MITCHELL LIBRARY

A pair of tidy bark-roofed homes: the one above, at Peak Hill, NSW, housed a miner and his family; the log house left was constructed in the American style at Bindi, in the Gippsland district of Victoria, by a settler who may himself have come from the United States.
LATROBE LIBRARY

These hardy pioneers may have improved their bush home with a corrugated roof in place of a leaky bark covering, but the wooden flue of their chimney needs occasional repair and replacement.
LATROBE LIBRARY

same splitters for 12s. 6d. Being myself an expert mechanic, the job of dressing and laying them down formed part of my work, as well as making and putting in glazed window sashes where the shutter holes had been, and a decent door in place of the hurdles on end with the spaces filled up with a few extra bars. [24]

The last important component of a slab hut was the bark roof. If speed and economy were essential, the best procedure was to build the entire hut of bark, which was far less complicated than slab walling.

Bark was often gathered and sold by the sheet. The *Yass Courier* reported on 17 December 1864: 'Some of the thieving fraternity have again victimised Mr West. This time it is not five tame and plump steers and heifers that have disappeared, but 120 sheets of stringy-bark, valued at 1s 6d a sheet.' These sheets were large and heavy, each representing quite a bit of labour, as this description makes clear:

in the centre room, while I was building up one of the compartments which had been left unfinished until bad weather, such as we have just had, should confine us to the house, and in-door occupations.' [22]

Properly compacted and surfaced with bullock's blood or linseed oil, earth floors were solid and serviceable, but if they were not properly prepared there could be problems — like those experienced by John Everett in 1838, in his hut near Guyra on the New England tablelands:

'On entering mind the step,' he warned, 'for though the earthern floor was level with the door sill at first, the frequent brushings out have sunk it not a little, and I expect if we lived in here very long we should sink it so low that we should not be able to look over the door sill.' [23]

As a result, unsatisfactory earth floors were replaced as soon as possible:

The first thing to do in the way of improvements was to cover the earthen floor of the hut with smoothly dressed slabs bedded on the earth, for which purpose a hundred were split for us by the

The method of barking the tree is to ring it at the butt, and again eight or nine feet above, then split it down from one girdle to the other, get the fingers in and start it from the wood. When once started, it will readily peel around the body of the tree, and come off in one whole sheet, eight feet long and from three to six feet wide. Take a long-handled shovel and strip off the round outside bark, and it will resemble a side of sole leather. Two men can strip from forty to sixty sheets in a day, so it did not take long to strip enough bark to cover a house, sides, roof and all. I have known houses built of bark in this way to last for ten or twelve years. The young stringy bark trees make the best of poles, and one can cut them twenty-five or thirty feet long, as straight as a candle, and, if desired, not more than three inches in diameter. Two men can go into the bush and strip the bark, cut the poles and put up a house inside a week, and a good tidy-looking one too, and such a one as many thousands who are worth their thousands of pounds have lived in for years. [25]

Bark was usually heated over a fire to soften the

Above: using the settler's standard tools and materials — an axe, a crosscut saw, a froe and a plentiful supply of greenhide — a bark hut could be erected with a day or two's concentrated effort.
LATROBE LIBRARY

Left: pride and determination shine in the faces of these Irish farmers at Port Fairy, Vic, working to expunge still-fresh memories of the famines that drove them to emigrate.
PORT FAIRY HISTORICAL SOCIETY

resin, then the sheets were laid flat in stacks and weighted to prevent warping.

When constructing a roof the first layer of bark was tied to the frame with greenhide thongs, which passed through holes mortised near the edge of each sheet. A second layer of bark was placed so that it covered the joints beneath, and above this an arrangement of poles called 'riders' was assembled. The riders were hinged at the ridge so they simply held down the bark with their own weight. The final detail was the ridge capping, which consisted of sheets of bark left to curl naturally.

So widespread were these building traditions that they became part of Australia's folklore, handed down in songs such as 'Stringy Bark and Greenhide':

If you want to build a hut to keep out wind and
*   weather,*
Stringy bark will make it snug and keep it all
*   together.*
Greenhide if it's used by you will make it all the
*   stronger,*
For if you tie it with greenhide, it's sure to last the
*   longer.*

Stringy bark and greenhide, that will never fail yer,
Stringy bark and greenhide, the mainstay of
*   Australia.*

Although the materials and construction techniques gave a certain uniformity of style to slab-and-bark houses, the interiors were as varied as the circumstances of their occupants. A slab house could become a very comfortable home if lined inside with milled timber and painted or stained. *The Australian Enquirer* in its chapter on slab huts concluded that ladies 'having little else to do' could possibly be occupied in this manner:

One of the prettiest decorations for a room is with paint and brown stain, the latter being extended a few feet up the wall and above it some pale tint in paint. Floors also look well if nicely stained and polished; they can be done in two shades if preferred, a centre square in light, the outer in very dark. In such climates as Queensland and some parts of New South Wales, stained floors are preferable on account of their being so cool. Many people imagine that a lady cannot stain and polish a room herself; that it requires a man's strength. This is not true. A persevering, energetic woman can and will do almost everything a man can, and in decorating a room a woman is thoroughly in her element.[26]

Certainly Rachel Henning worked hard decorating the many houses she occupied. In a letter from her brother Biddulph's slab homestead Exmoor, in Queensland, she triumphantly records:

We have got the room papered at last. We finished it yesterday, Biddulph and I and Annie and Mr Hedgeland. We did about half each, and it really looks very well considering that it is extremely difficult to paper over strained canvas, much more so than over a good, firm plastered wall. The paper is an extremely pretty one, a very light green ground with a small white pattern of wild roses and ivy-leaves on it. I am afraid it is the true arsenic green, but in this airy abode I do not think we are likely to be poisoned. It is the greatest improvement to the house and sitting-room. There is paper enough for all the rooms, but I do not think we are likely to undertake any more at present. Our room is lined with white calico, and Biddulph does not care about doing his own or the rest.

The house is so comfortable now that it is all floored and lined. We have a chest of drawers, too, in our room, which is a great convenience. You hardly know how much till you have had some months' experience of 'rooting' in boxes for your things. Four looking-glasses have likewise been set up in the different rooms. We have a large one with a marble stand wherein I have discovered the interesting fact that I look very ancient and Annie more so under the influence of the hot climate, though it agrees so well with me.[27]

The furniture of rural houses sometimes consisted of 'mahogany tables, chairs and sideboards, etc., and the other moveables of a respectable family in town'. Anne Baxter, in *Memories of the*

Past, describes the interior of Commissioner Mac-Donald's hut in New England in 1843:

His domicile was a small hut of three rooms, very badly finished outside, but when you went inside you felt quite astonished how very snug a building of the sort may be made . . .

The drawing-room furnished so well, and on a round table in the centre of the room annuals placed on it in such a tasty manner, and five good engravings hanging on the walls. The dining-room was covered with oil-cloth and on either side of the fire-place was a nice collection of books. The bedroom was small but very comfortable; the toilette-table prettily ornamented with articles in silver, crystal and china; and three paintings of exceedingly pretty female forms, nicely framed and well hung, showing the owner to be a man of taste.[28]

In more remote areas almost everything was handmade:

Bullock and goat hides were carefully pegged and salted and later softened by patient rubbing with rough stones to make floor mats and bed coverings. This was work at which the black women excelled, sitting for hours in the shade pounding away in the ancient manner of crushing the hard nardoo.

The furniture was solid and rough-hewn, the bunks of unplaned timber and rawhide, the big dining table built in the main room so that it could never be removed in one piece.[29]

Some furniture was of a more temporary nature. Alexander Harris, describing a squatter's first bark home, said that in the middle

was a little table, and that too was of bark, to wit, a sheet about 3 feet one way by 2 the other, nailed on

In a desperate attempt to soften the rawness of life in the bush, settlers' wives created havens of Victorian correctness in slab huts whose interior walls were sometimes lined with painted hessian.
MITCHELL LIBRARY

Four stages in the surprisingly rapid evolution of a squatter's home, from D.E. Cooper's 'Challicum Sketchbook.' *Above:* taking possession of their land, the Coopers live under canvas at Challicum, northwest of Bendigo, in early 1842. *Right:* the Cooper's first slab-huts were built later in 1842 to protect the men from the rugged winter of northern Victoria.

Above: additions in 1843 resulted in a comfortable and respectable farmhouse (note the paling fence around the 'home paddock'). *Left:* by 1845 the station homestead was surrounded by the earlier homes, now relegated to the status of outbuildings.
NATIONAL LIBRARY OF AUSTRALIA

to four little posts driven into the ground, and having of course its inner or smooth side upways. The architect of the building has used all his materials whilst they were green, so that in seasoning they had twisted into all manner of forms except planes: and as is usually the case the worst example came from the most responsible quarter: the table was the crookedest thing in the whole hut, not excepting the dog's hind leg. Standing about the floor were sundry square-ended round blocks of wood, just as they were first sawn off the tree transversely: they were each about eighteen inches long, and their official rank in the domestic system was equivalent to that of the civilised chair.[30]

In her travels Rachel Henning noticed some other unusual homemade chairs, in Queensland:

Mr Hedgeland has just been making for the verandah two of the easy-chairs called 'squatter's delights'. They are made of two straight poles, which are leant against the wall of the house ladder-wise. These are held together by two crossbars, and to the bars is nailed a strip of strong canvas, such as we use for wool-bagging, and this forms the seat and back of the chair. The materials are simple enough, but I think it is the most comfortable kind of easy-chair I know.[31]

Success on the land would see this two-legged leaning seat replaced by the traditional 'squatter's chair', an unwieldy but comfortable piece of verandah furniture with arms that extended for 1.5 metres or so to allow the sitter to put his feet up.

With additions such as these, the slab houses of the squatters and selectors gradually developed into comfortable well-furnished homes surrounded by gardens fenced with split palings, creating a tradition of rural architecture that was to last well into the twentieth century.

Meanwhile, the houses of the city dwellers were developing a style of their own.

'Colonial Fashions' 1860-1880

*Sydney has improved in several important points during the two years of
my sojourn at the Antipodes. Its increase is enormous; for a new suburb, connecting
Darlinghurst with the city by one continuous street, half a mile long, with numerous
lateral branches, has sprung up where, two years ago, the belated diner-out might
have fallen among bushrangers, and the bewildered one might have fallen into
a blind ditch, and there bivouacked with the frogs 'until
daylight did appear'.*

Colonel Charles Mundy, 1848

ALTHOUGH IT WAS THE SQUATTERS, SELECTORS and miners who were the real sources of the colony's wealth, the tangible evidence of Australia's newfound prosperity could best be seen in the cities, where most of the money was spent.

Once survival ceases to be a problem the next priority is comfort and, after that, fashion. By the 1860s, 'Colonial' fashions in dress, social behaviour and housing began to influence those who could afford them. The style of one's home became an important consideration to the emerging middle class, and the building industry boomed.

Some observers thought it was high time Australians moved away from the influence of the mother country and developed houses that were more appropriate. One was Charles Mundy, who wrote in 1848:

Sydney is, I think, more exclusively English in its population than either Liverpool or London. Were it not for an occasional orange-tree in full bloom or fruit in the back yard of some of the older cottages, or a flock of little green parrots whistling as they alight for a moment on a housetop, one might fancy himself at Brighton or Plymouth.

The construction of the buildings is blameably ill-suited to a semi-tropical climate — barefaced, smug-looking tenements, without verandahs or even broad eaves, a fault extending to the Government House itself, whose great staring windows are doomed to grill unveiled, because, forsooth, any excrescence upon their stone mullions would

be heterodox to the order or disorder of its architecture. Surely a little composite licence might have been allowable in such a case and climate.[1]

As a visitor, Mundy was unaware that there were other factors responsible for the lack of adequate shading devices on the older houses in the city. Early Sydney had simply grown organically. With few effective attempts at building control, many wooden shops, houses, and warehouses pressed against each other, creating a potential fire hazard that worried authorities.

In an attempt to deal with this problem, the Legislative Council of New South Wales introduced comprehensive building regulations in January 1838. Based on the London Building Act of 1709, the regulations banned the use of shingles, bark, or thatching for roofs and prohibited the use of timber closer than 4 inches (10 centimetres) to the face of a building. Fireproof party walls were another requirement.

The immediate effects were the demolition of verandahs and the disappearance of roof overhangs as walls were carried up past the eaves line to form a parapet. Despite much public protest the age of uniformity, defined by regulation, had begun.

The Gothic style, which originated in Britain, bred another sort of conformity — that of fashion. The Gothic Revival provided some light relief from the austerity of Georgian design, even in the simple suburban cottage where several of the characteristics of the larger Gothic mansions of the rich were adopted on a smaller scale.

The drawing room was extended forward to present an asymmetrical front, the gable roof was pitched high and the gable edges decorated with carved bargeboards. The roof was hipped and extended to cover a small wooden entry porch. Double-hung and casement windows, which had recently become available, were incorporated into the design, providing more light to the interior.

For those who couldn't afford the luxury of a detached cottage, a double or single-storey terrace was an economical alternative. These were a favourite with speculators, since they required a much smaller site per unit and were considerably cheaper to build. The common dividing walls represented a substantial saving in materials, the repetitive design was easy for builders to work with, and the roofs and fencing were continuous.

A typical larger terrace had a 4.8-metre frontage on a block of land roughly 36 metres long. One in Paddington, offered for sale by Sydney real estate agents Richardson and Wrench in 1877, was described as being 'built of brick on stone, with a small garden plot, verandah and balcony in front, hall, 5 large rooms, kitchen with range, pantry, a weatherboard bathroom, wash-house with copper and tubs, wood and fowl house, well of water and garden at rear'.

The terrace facades were almost always ornamented with cast iron, the factory-produced equivalent of hand-wrought iron. Although the cast iron was imported from England, it was cheap, plentiful and fashionable. So fashionable, in fact, that by the 1870s several Australian factories were producing local designs and patterns which remain distinctive features of many inner-city suburbs today.

Both local and imported building materials were readily available. The *Sydney Morning Herald* in 1859 carried columns of advertisements for Baltic and American flooring, dressed and rough sawn weatherboards, slates, galvanised iron for flat and curved roofs, doors, windows, colonial hardwoods and, of course, red cedar, probably the most popular timber available:

The stranger is much struck by the handsome appearance given by the profuse use of cedar in the fittings of the Sydney dwellings. The doors and sashes, the window-frames and shutters, staircases and balustrades, skirting-boards and cornices, and, in a few instances, the floors and ceilings, are all of cedar. It has all the beauty in colour and figure of the Spanish mahogany; indeed, the experience of an upholsterer is necessary to detect the difference by sight alone.[2]

Attracting the attention of an experienced upholsterer was no easy task — they were too busy creating over-stuffed couches and sofas to fill the new drawing rooms:

Many of the private residences of Sydney and its suburbs are both handsome and comfortable — most of them crowded with expensive furniture, therein differing from the practice in most warm countries, where the receiving-rooms and bedrooms contain little beyond the muniments necessary for sitting and lying, and those of the plainest, hardest, and most undraped description.[3]

The author of a letter from Adelaide in 1853 describes the interior of the cottage of a Mr Allen as 'brimming with snug English comfort'. Pride of place often went to the piano, a popular item for genteel home entertainment:

The Parlour contained a neat little Broadwood, a trifle the worse for the late hot winds, and jingling accordingly; the mantel piece was garnished with elegant nick-nackeries, and I observed crochet books lying about the room. It is strange to find such luxuries at the Antipodes, and plenty of them, for there seemed to be pianofortes in half the houses in Adelaide.[4]

A piano was certainly an important piece of furniture in the Elliott family home at Jeffcott Street, North Adelaide. In a remarkably long and detailed letter to his mother, written in 1860, journalist Joseph Elliott painted a unique picture of suburban life.

The single-fronted stone cottage the Elliotts rented had a simple floor plan, one that can be seen

A cheerful group of suburban swells, complete with dog and penny-farthing bicycle, pose for the camera in Ballarat in 1875. The cast iron on the verandah is in simple unjoined sections.
MUSEUM OF VICTORIA

The cluttered drawing
room of James Chisholm's
home in George Street,
Sydney, is very much in
the English style (copied
from Queen Victoria's
Balmoral retreat) of the
late 1870s.
MUSEUM OF VICTORIA

Gothic tracery adorns the brand-new Burwood, Sydney, home of Eugene Nicolle (seen standing in the no doubt cool shadow of his front verandah), the pioneer of refrigeration in Australia.
NATIONAL LIBRARY

Above: Surrounded by a disproportionately grand brick-and-iron fence, this comfortable Bendigo residence of 1861 sports a similarly incongruous mixture of Gothic, Neoclassical and Italianate detailing.
LATROBE LIBRARY

Right: an elegant Gothic house at the corner of Annandale Street and Loftus Road in the select eastern Sydney suburb of Darling Point. Photographed in 1877, it remains in use today.
MITCHELL LIBRARY

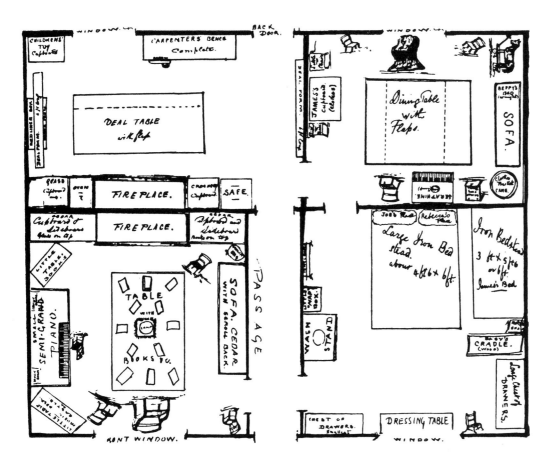

repeated consistently in small Australian houses — four rooms divided by a central passage. The first room on the left was the parlour, where visitors were received and entertained. As the showplace of the house it contained the best furniture, all of polished cedar. On display, carefully arranged on tables, were the Elliotts' motley collection of heirlooms, souvenirs, and conversation pieces such as the 'coagulated glass and china vases that were dissolved and run into each other very beautifully at a great fire at the Port some years ago'.[5]

The white-painted walls were crowded with family portraits and George Baxter colour prints (which closely resembled oil paintings) of British heroes such as the Duke of Wellington, Nelson and Robert Peel. Leather-bound books and cutglass decanters covered the sideboards, but pride of place went to a bizarre model castle made of cardboard covered with shells and coloured sand. There was a space in the middle for a lamp or

candle so that 'the light will then only proceed out of the windows and doors'. Just the thing for a lively evening's entertainment.

Across the passage was the bedroom where Joseph and his wife Rebecca slept on a large iron bedstead, with their young son James on a small bed close by. There was not much room left. Around the walls were two chests of drawers, a dressing table and a washstand with a floral pottery jug and basin.

An adjoining door led to the sitting room, where their daughter Rebecca slept on a sofa. The room was dominated by a large dropside dining table, where the family occasionally gathered for formal meals. Against one wall was a seraphine or harmonium (a variety of small treadle organ), a bargain Joseph had picked up somewhere. After spending weeks restoring it he felt that it was 'a very nice instrument with but one fault and that is the worst and greatest fault it could possibly have — viz bad notes'.[6]

Joseph Elliott's proud and detailed sketch plan of the interior of his house, here reconstructed from four separate drawings. Every room in this tidy cottage was made to serve at least two purposes.
STATE LIBRARY OF SA

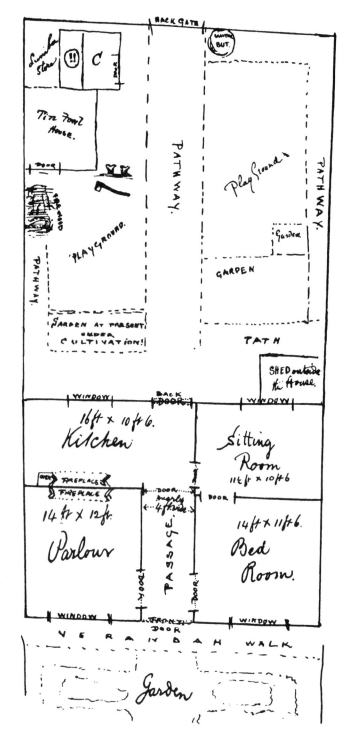

A reconstruction of Joseph Elliott's plan of his home and garden in Jeffcott Street, Adelaide. His children, James and Rebecca, had ample play room between the house and the backyard WC, coyly marked 'C' on the plan.
STATE LIBRARY OF SA

Since the Elliotts had no servants, the centre of the family's daily life was the kitchen, which opened on to the backyard. Most meals were eaten around the deal table with its homemade extension flap. There were no chairs; the family sat on simple utilitarian benches which could also serve a variety of purposes, as did the kitchen itself. Baths were taken there, the washing tubs and other odd kitchen equipment being stored in the shed at the rear of the sitting room.

Although the other rooms were carpeted, the floor of the kitchen was 'what is called concrete, being a composition of three parts sand and one part lime, which when properly set becomes as hard as a rock'.[7] Perishable food was kept in the large, homemade flyproof safe with walls of perforated zinc sheet:

It has a zinc front and two sides and all the corners of wood are closely joined and covered with tin. It is painted dark green, looks a regular serviceable article, has three shelves inside and is used for eatables requiring air but not too much of it ... It stands on four little feet so that if necessary they could be placed in water tins to prevent ants getting inside.[8]

Cooking was on an open fire using cast-iron cooking pots, or in the oven, which was heated by a second fire on the right of the wide fireplace. The oven was simply 'one of these large iron kegs bricked in and a shelf put inside. It bakes first rate. We send no meat etc. to the Baker's to bake and sometimes we have some nice home-made bread.'[9] The brickwork around the oven and fireplace was polished with black lead (graphite). On the cedar mantelpiece old ginger jars held coffee and tea, while crockery and glassware were kept in cupboards on each side.

The backyard, fenced with split palings, contained the woodpile, children's play area and fowl house. Water — stored in a large wooden cask near the back gate — was delivered at a cost of about 2 shillings for 50 gallons (around 220 litres) and carried in buckets to the house.

Hidden discreetly behind the fowl house was the

'convenience'. Joseph asks with Victorian delicacy:

Shall I tell you what the place that is marked 'C' is? How rude you are, most likely you'll say. But if I omitted to mention it, you might think we did without, as they do up in the bush here, for not one in a dozen or twenty have such conveniences!! Ah! Ah! I know you're laughing and cannot help it — nor can I.[10]

Joseph's mirth notwithstanding, urban sanitation in the 1860s was no laughing matter. The typical outhouse was a small building placed as far from the house as possible, usually close to the back gate so the night-cart workers could have easy access. If the block of land was large enough, burial of the night soil on one's own property was often permitted. Chamber pots kept under beds during the night also needed to be emptied.

The practice of burying waste led to a boom in the planting of citrus trees. These performed a dual role: they responded well to the fertiliser and,

importantly, marked the position of the latest hole so that no one stepped on it.

In less ideal situations there were no such warnings. In old, closely settled suburbs like Sydney's Rocks district, no orderly system of waste disposal existed and effluent was simply discharged into the street. Despite this, parts of the Rocks had a charm of their own. William Stanley Jevons, taking a stroll on the warm evening of 10 November 1858, left a brief but graphic picture of the scene:

In the lighter parts of the Rocks, Gloucester and Cumberland Streets, there [were] ... a few people gossiping at the corners, or moving homewards. Princes Street was perfectly quiet except for the subdued murmur of conversation inside the dwellings ... [which] was in almost every part of the town audible. The interior of all the dwellings too, with few exceptions, appeared cheerful where a glimpse could be obtained. The family was gener-

Old techniques mingle with new technology in this early 1870s cottage at Ballarat, Vic. Clad with milled weather board, it has a hand-split paling fence and a roof of pressed metal sheets.
MUSEUM OF VICTORIA

Above: Cumberland Street in Sydney's Rocks district would have looked much like this to William Jevons as he strolled on warm summer evenings in 1858; some of these houses are still standing.

Right: the Rocks survived as a living museum of house styles purely because it was such a benighted slum that developers had no desire to 'improve' the oldest remaining part of early Sydney.

ally round the central table or sitting about on chairs and sofa. The females were generally engaged in needlework; all were talking.[11]

Jevons also pointed out that, despite building regulations, the condition of Sydney's new inner-city working class suburbs — like the estate of Dr Redfern, and the Waterloo estate of Sir Daniel Cooper — left much to be desired. Needless to say, the owners did not live there but retired with their profits to more salubrious locations overlooking the harbour, leaving the poor to fend for themselves.

Nowhere perhaps except in Australia could be seen collections of such hastily erected frail small habitations, devoid of even a pretence to ornament and in many or most cases belonging to, and built by those who inhabit them. Almost every labourer and mechanic here has his own residence or

freehold or leasehold land and unpretending as it is to any conveniences or beauties, it yet satisfies him better than the brick built, closely packed and rented houses of English towns. An Australian second or third class suburb would not be taken for a permanent part of a town at all; it more resembles the wooden huts of a military encampment. In a great majority of cases the first plan only includes two small rooms, to which others are sometimes added afterwards; no two designs are alike and the materials are most various. I might enumerate many kinds of them, such as with 1. Slabs or logs of wood, 2. Palings or split wood, 3. Canvas, 4. Weatherboards, 5. Tongued and grooved boards, 6. Plain or corrugated sheets of iron or other metal; 7. Bricks, 8. Brick and wood combined, 9. Rubble stone, 10. Lathe and plaster, 11. Ashlar stone work, etc. I have seen some houses into which broken iron stone, and glass bottles enter as a component,

Making bricks for a new homestead on a western New South Wales property. Brickmakers would have supervised the work, but the owner's family and station hands would also have pitched in.
LATROBE LIBRARY

95

Above: refugees in their own land, these Victorian Aborigines cover their shelters with 'gubba' blankets, handed out by a condescending government, and themselves with cast-off clothes.
STATE LIBRARY OF TASMANIA

Right: more to white tastes was the lifestyle of the Kanakas, the kidnapped or indentured Melanesians who worked in the canefields of Queensland, and who build eminently practical high-set houses.
JOHN OXLEY LIBRARY

while both the old wood and sheet tin of packing cases is largely made use of, the latter especially for roofs. Split wooden shingles are almost always used for roofing, but corrugated and plain sheet iron, patent zinc tiles, sheets of bark, or proper slates are also used. All these modes of construction may be seen in close succession and often even combined in one house in such suburbs as Redfern and Waterloo Estate and the resulting mass of dwellings have the most comfortless and unpicturesque appearance imaginable. [12]

Although the labourers' houses may have lacked some creature comforts, another social group, living in far worse conditions, excited little comment for the simple reason that its members were black. 'Urban' Aborigines — those who had been dispossessed of their land in order to create the suburban subdivisions that made the vendors rich and kept the purchasers under mortgage for the rest of their lives — remained bound to their land by religious beliefs which were and still are part of their traditional way of life.

Each tribal group had its own territory, which it was often happy to share with the thankless white newcomers. For city blacks it was a one-sided bargain: since other tribes would resent any permanent resettlement, their only option was to camp in makeshift shanties around the new cities and towns, surviving as best they could.

In some rural areas this led to conflict, but in others there was at least an understanding of the dilemma. Queensland pioneer Mary Banks wrote concerning their property in the Brisbane Valley:

This tribe never molested our cattle or our sheep. Its right to camp in the old haunts, to hunt kangaroos, opossums and fish, and to hold the Bunya-nut feast on the hill were respected and it respected my father's property in return. If a tribe were chased away from its native district, its own place on the river or among the hills, there was no place for it anywhere else. The surrounding country belonged to other tribes, who allowed no trespasser on their preserves; the displaced tribe became outcast and homeless and often died miser-

ably. The first settler knew nothing of these tribal laws, of the totem's home, or the virtue pertaining to certain places. [13]

Although settlers in the remote Brisbane Valley may have been ignorant of Aboriginal lore, they were certainly familiar with the Gothic Revival. Charles Allen, travelling through the valley on his way to the northern goldfields in 1867, found this hard to believe in such a far-flung outpost of Empire:

In many instances, you are forcibly struck with the absurd manner in which English architecture is copied ...

On arriving at Ipswich, I was astonished to see, perched on a hill-top, a red-brick Gothic building, with the high pitched roof and narrow windows which characterise such buildings in cold countries. Not only were there no verandahs, to protect from the sun's rays, but the bedrooms were upstairs, just under the roof, and, having scarcely any windows, were hardly ever cool. [14]

Whether it was appropriate or not, Gothic Revival found its spired and heavily mullioned way into every part of Australia. Here it ignores the climate of Dawson Valley, Brisbane, in 1867. JOHN OXLEY LIBRARY

In the days before insulation there was value in building as lightly as possible, taking advantage of the north's equable winters. The exposed studs of the 1870s low-stumped Queensland homestead above have been formed into a decorative diamond pattern.
Right: another solution to the extremes of the Queensland climate was to raise the building a little further, promoting cool breezes underneath, and to add a ventilator to allow hot air trapped beneath the corrugated iron roof to escape.
JOHN OXLEY LIBRARY

Nor was Allen particularly impressed with what he saw farther north. After a visit to Gympie, he wrote:

On landing in an Australian town, the traveller is certainly not struck by any great beauty in the houses; nor do they appear as though the owners studied the picturesque, or even the comfortable, in their domestic architecture. Every man builds, upon the allotment which he buys, just what kind of house or cottage he chooses. In the Queensland towns these are mostly wooden or iron constructions, raised on piles, and consisting of a single floor, with a small verandah in front. The size depends upon the requirements or the purse of the settler, and as no two are alike, it gives the newly-formed town an irregular appearance, not very pleasing to the eye.[15]

Although it may not have appealed to his aesthetic sensibilities, Allen was in fact witnessing the beginning of a unique style which was to become favoured throughout northern Australia — the high-set house.

These lightly framed timber buildings, sitting on 1.5 to 2-metre-high stumps made from tree trunks, represented the first real attempt to create houses appropriate to the climate. At the same time, advances in the technology of timber construction helped to simplify the building process.

Prior to the Industrial Revolution nails were expensive hand-forged items which builders used sparingly, preferring instead to use neat mortise-and-tenon joints and wooden pegs to secure house frames. But the new factory-produced wire nails were so cheap that they could be used freely, and many builders abandoned the time-consuming practices of the past in favour of housed or butt joints held together by skew nailing.

Coincidentally, the shortage of timber in Britain had led tradesmen there to experiment with house frames built of lighter timbers. Since this practice also reduced building costs, it quickly found favour

Ready for a sweltering soiree, the score for the waltz 'Tout a Vous' sits on the piano in a north Queensland home decorated in the cool and informal tropical style of the 1880s.
JOHN OXLEY LIBRARY

99

with speculative builders everywhere, especially in the United States. Many orthodox builders were disgusted by the idea, however, because of the lack of skill required:

A cheaper method of constructing these houses is sometimes adopted, with thinner timbers and practically no framed joints, all the connections being made by means of nailing. This is locally known as balloon framing, in humorous reference to their lightness … This work is 'jerry' of the worst description, and no further particulars of it are considered necessary.[16]

By the 1860s the balloon frame was used by many carpenters working on cheaper forms of housing. William Howitt remarked on this in Melbourne in 1855:

The timbers of which their skeletons are first formed are often only two inches by two and a half in thickness. I actually measured some in Colling-wood — the spars and joists about two inches by three. The floors are generally raised about a foot from the ground, and are principally supported by pegs driven into the ground, just as you see pegs driven to mark out the site of any intended building. The whole thing, before they cover it with boards, looks more like a spider's web, or a birds-cage, than anything else. You imagine you might just kick it over, as you would a basket.[17]

In Queensland, however, the balloon frame was to survive many a cyclone.

As Howitt observed, the practice of building on low stumps was already common in the south; in the tropics it had many advantages over building on the ground. The first was in combatting the voracious local termites, known as white ants. Termites are formidable, capable of eating through several layers of sheet lead in order to reach their goal — wood of any kind, preferably softwood. Their presence is often undetected until too late:

Above: an early high-stumped house at Thomas Swallow's Hambledon plantation, south of Cairns. Bedrooms were upstairs, kitchen and living room downstairs, and the water tank (left) kept cool in the shade.
CAIRNS HISTORICAL SOCIETY

Facing page
In a sensible colonial adaptation of the Swiss chalet, the 'under-the-house', or ground floor, of this owner-built Queenslander is used as a stables and tackroom for station horses.

101

Fretwork detailing such as this over the entrance of a Springhill, Brisbane, house — such a distinctive feature of Queensland houses — was just beginning to appear when this photograph was taken in the 1870s. JOHN OXLEY LIBRARY

I have seen wooden doors and window frames left mere shells, the termites having eaten all the soft wood, avoiding the hard notches, and leaving about one sixteenth of an inch of the outside wood. To all appearances, the woodwork is as sound as ever.[18]

The consequences could be structurally disastrous, as one poet observed in a short ditty familiar to Queenslanders:

*Some primal termite knocked on wood
And tasted it and found it good,
And that is why your Aunty May
Fell through the kitchen floor today.*

The first recorded instance of high stumps on houses in Australia was at Port Essington (near the present site of Darwin) in 1838. One of the settlers, George Windsor Earl, had observed the high-set houses of the Malays in the East Indies. These are traditionally built with wooden stumps which are easily replaceable, a quality which also proved effective at Port Essington, since it was mentioned in a report that the 'temporary method of piling in order to raise the buildings has proved very useful. Had they been fixed to the ground in the usual manner, they must have been destroyed long since'.[19] The prefabricated Port Essington buildings were raised 2.5 metres above the ground so

that it was easy to walk underneath and 'observe and check the attacks of these destructive insects'.

It seems unlikely that this concept was communicated to Queensland from that source because the early houses there were usually on much shorter stumps. The operator of the telegraph station at Junction Creek, Queensland, complained sadly in his report of 1874:

The white ants are causing considerable damage to these buildings and I see no way of checking them as the blocks are too low to allow a person to get under the house. The kitchen and water closet will not last this wet season.

Common sense soon provided the solution. Increasing the height of the stumps also exposed the house and verandah to the breeze as well as providing cool insulated space at ground level. A traveller on the lower Herbert River in north Queensland remarked of one settlement:

The dwelling house is substantially built on high piles, a peculiarity, by-the-by, everywhere noticeable. It might be thought to be suggestive of floods, but on enquiry it appears that by building in this manner, cool and airy dining rooms and store rooms are provided.[20]

The verandah was another essential component

Having seen his entire wardrobe reduced to 'little more than ... heaps of mud and buttons' by termites, Mr V.L. Solomon kept them at bay with a shield of corrugated iron in his new Darwin home.
NATIONAL LIBRARY OF AUSTRALIA

Halfway between a tent and a house, this north Queensland selector's dwelling provided shelter while the backbreaking work of clearing 'useless' scrub went on in preparation for farming.
LATROBE LIBRARY

of the Queensland style. In plan a typical house had a central core of four rooms surrounded by a wide verandah. The uninsulated and often unventilated iron roof did not produce comfortable conditions inside, so most family life took place out on the verandah, shifting from place to place during the day to avoid the sun. At night it was often the coolest place to sleep, with a mosquito net carefully tucked in for protection from the abundant tropical insect life.

Sometimes sleeping areas were partially enclosed, such as those on John Moffat's house at Irvinebank near Cairns:

As up to the present our living accommodation consisted of five 6 x 8 tents and a little hut for feeding in, we went in at once for a respectable house built on 8 feet stumps; the house for residence purposes and the space underneath for working in and stores ... upstairs we have a sitting room 16 x 14, two bedrooms 10 x 8 and the makings of four verandah bedrooms each 8 x 7½, with front verandah, from which a nice view of the dam is had. On the ground we have fine [or five] cool rooms for offices, stores, assaying room etc.[21]

Verandahs had many other possibilities:

a recreation centre, playground for the young on wet days, store room and vantage point for surveying the scenery or passers-by. Suspended from its rafters were the meat safe, the water bag, the clothesline for wet weather, swings for the children, bird cages, the Christmas hams and numerous pieces of wire or hooks on which to hang hats and overcoats.

Along the walls rows of nails or pegs carried an assortment of objects from guns to stockwhips and schoolbags.

If the spelling of the word occasioned some hardship to the young it had its compensations in other ways, not least of which was the shelter it provided for the menagerie of animals which seemed to accompany the pioneer household.[22]

The walls of better quality houses were frequently clad on the inside only with sawn weatherboards, leaving the diagonally braced, sawn timber frame exposed on the exterior. Others had walls of corrugated iron. Whichever style was chosen, the construction of a house was not seen as a major problem:

The houses in Bowen are all built of wood, and a very easy affair it is for anyone to build them.

Photographed in the 1880s, To Kalon, an Ingham sugar-planter's home, has a massive thatched roof copied from the colonial bungalows of the Raj; its source is less than surprising, given the Indian connections of many planters.
FRYER LIBRARY

105

Gogg's Terrace in Ipswich was a well-designed attempt at multiple housing, but terraces failed to catch the popular imagination in Queensland, where land was generally cheap.
JOHN OXLEY LIBRARY

Indeed house building in the small Queensland towns can scarcely be called a trade, insomuch that any practical man who can use carpenter's tools could easily build his own house.[23]

Since the climate was similar to other tropical British colonies, it seemed logical to borrow some ideas on design and construction. Charles Allen mentioned one example:

I stayed many months in a Queensland bungalow, built somewhat after the model of those in India, and which may be taken as a type of the best of the bush houses; although many large stations are on a much more extensive scale. In this one the front half of the house, instead of being divided into two or more rooms, consists of one large room, with glass doors at either end and all along the front, so that a current of air always blows through it; and this model might be followed with advantage,

although it is not yet very common. An Anglo-Indian lady, who was her own architect, is the owner of this pretty residence.[24]

For a woman to be her own architect in the 1860s was certainly irregular. Indeed, the authors of *Working Drawings and Designs in Architecture and Building* were being rather avant-garde when they suggested that an architect should, on occasion, seek a female's advice:

It might seem, at first sight, beneath the dignity of an architect to take counsel — while engaged in planning a house — from a housewife ... There are few houses built ... the arrangements and conveniences of which could not be modified with advantage after taking a housewife — who knows what work there is in a house to do, and how to do it — through all its apartments, and asking her opinion about them; how far they are calculated to pro-

mote or hinder economy and convenience ... *Doubtless it will be objected that there will be difficulty in getting such a counsellor to understand the intricacies of a plan. But this ... understanding of a plan by the female mind, is not after all so difficult a matter as is, or might be, supposed.*[25]

In the early days there was little work in Queensland for architects, condescending or otherwise, but a period of rapid growth soon brought about many changes.

With an influx of overseas capital to promote development of its resources, Queensland in the 1870s was the State most favoured by immigrants, who arrived in their thousands to provide an enthusiastic labour force. By the early 1880s, a boom was under way, financed by the income from gold, sugar and pastoral industries. Suddenly Queensland was no longer a frontier colony but a prosperous State keen to display its wealth.

The Queensland house was due for a facelift.

'A Wilderness of Villas' 1880-1900

One of the first features which strike the atttention of the stranger
approaching Brisbane, especially by the river, is the architecture of the dwelling
houses. The prevailing style is, with modifications, that of the Indian bungalow —
a single, sometimes double, storeyed cottage, generally of wood, with pyramidal roof, and
surrounded by broad verandahs, upon which open many french doors or low windows.
Closed in by bamboo curtains or Venetians, furnished with hammocks, ample cane
lounges and easy chairs, the verandah is on summer evenings the most important
tributary to the comfort of a house. By keeping off the heat of the sun's
rays from windows and walls, it enables a house to be kept cool and
open to the sea breeze, which, blowing from the north-east,
is the great temperer of the summer heat.

Cassell's Picturesque Australasia 1888

THE WAVES OF IMMIGRANTS TO SOUTHERN QUEENS-land during the 1880s helped to increase the population of Brisbane to well over 100 000, and suburbs and housing estates proliferated. As in other capital cities, this expansion was facilitated by the introduction of an efficient public transport system of railways and trams.

The timber houses in these new suburbs began to develop a distinctive style, derived from the high-stumped homes of early settlement. In hilly areas the stumps provided a simple solution to the building problems associated with steep sites. The level platform of the house was simply supported on a timber framework secured to stumps that varied in length according to the slope of the land: a very hilly site might have stumps 1 metre high at one end and 7 metres at the other.

The basic plan was of four rooms, with a verandah front and back joined by a central hallway and topped by a pyramid-shaped roof of galvanised iron (fast becoming the most popular roofing in the north). As always, there were critics:

These tin roofs, even with ceilings, which they don't always have, mean 105° Fahrenheit, indoors, at midsummer, and 35° of the same, at midnight, at midwinter. *'Awfully Jolly', as you must perceive, for typhoid fever in January, or pneumonia in July (as the case may be), and tends to rapid recovery, of course. But oh! for the children! the little Georges and the small Claras, born, and yet to be born, who, too, will have to inhabit, and to die in those same tin roof houses. Poor little pets! They will do their small and level best, you know, to embellish these death traps; they will collect fragments of looking-glass, bits of old, coloured china, scraps of gay ribbon, and sea shells, to 'make a play' with; and, like the 'bower bird' of Australia (their native land), they will do their utmost to draw, in their innocent baby play, and infant imagination, all the fairy fun that can be got out of a tin roof hut, on a swampy plot of 20 perches (or half that in the inner suburbs).*[1]

One person who would have agreed whole-heartedly with this outburst from Nehemiah Bartley was Judge G.W. Paul. During a stay in Kobe, Japan, in the 1870s the judge observed that the traditional houses there were more suited to Queensland than that country, where they became uncomfortably cold in the winter. He bought the 28-square-metre house he was living in as an example, and had it dismantled and sent to Bris-

Facing page
Corrugated-iron roofs turned the interiors of Darwin houses into ovens, so most activities took place on the verandah. Split bamboo screens provided welcome shade without blocking the breeze.
BATTYE LIBRARY

William Forbes' Cairns house, built around 1890, has symmetrical wooden verandah-post ornaments and a decorative balustrade. Note the ant-caps on top of the stumps.
JOHN OXLEY LIBRARY

bane, along with five Japanese tradesmen to re-build it. At his housewarming at New Farm in 1887, he remarked to a reporter that, 'apart from raising house stumps to escape the ravages of white ants, little has been done toward making Queensland homes suitable for Queensland requirements'. But, despite its climatic suitability, the Japanese style found no favour with a conservative public which preferred to modify the devil it knew.

Several measures were adopted in an attempt further to discourage termites. The wooden stumps were charred, immersed in salt water, or treated with tar or creosote to make them unpalatable. The stumps were capped with mass-produced dish-shaped caps made from 24-gauge galvanised iron, which forced the termites to build their galleries out into the open to get around the caps. This method, which is still used in many areas today, meant that the termites' presence was more easily observed and the galleries destroyed.

Although many builders and homeowners were content to leave the stained piers exposed, those with more refined sensibilities, such as architect Robin Dods, were appalled by 'these unsightly houses set on a forest of black stumps'. Dods himself designed a form of decorative enclosure to conceal them. Others used lattice or vertical timber battens to produce a more finished appearance. This, combined with the ornamental timber balustrade that usually surrounded the verandah, gave the suburban timber houses of Brisbane a charm enhanced by their luxuriant tropical gardens.

Farther south the effects of the boom were manifesting themselves in a slightly more frenetic manner. In Sydney, wrote James Inglis in 1880:

The overflow of bricks and mortar has spread like a lava-flood . . . till the houses now lie, pile on pile, tier on tier, and succeed each other row after row, street after street . . . Everywhere the sound of the workmen's tools is heard, all through the busy day. Brickyards are worked to their utmost capacity, iron foundries are taxed to their greatest powers, saw-mills and joinery establishments are in full activity, and at present the building trades are in constant and vigorous employment.[2]

PROTECTION AGAINST "WHITE ANTS."

No. 24.

As a protection against White Ants, any of these buildings can be raised about 3 ft. off the ground, on **"Rowell's"** Improved Iron Pillars with Vermin proof **"Inverted Cups."** Examples of this are given by illustrations Nos. 19 and 22.

The Cap and Base are interchangeable so that they may be fixed with Cup reversed for filling with liquid, if desired.

"ROWELL'S" IMPROVED IRON PILLAR FOR SUPPORTING BUILDINGS OFF THE GROUND.

Above: not every Queenslander needed (or, indeed, could afford) a high-stumped house. Often the main dwelling was raised just far enough for a laundry and storeroom to be built-in beneath.
JOHN OXLEY LIBRARY

Left: ant-caps were needed even for the iron posts of prefabricated houses. This model, offered by David Rowell and Co. of London, could be inverted and filled with poison as a further discouragement to pests.

Above: a desire for privacy (or, as here, for protection against the bracing breezes of seaside Coogee, Sydney) saw verandahs wholly or partially enclosed, with varying degrees of aesthetic success.
MITCHELL LIBRARY

Right: at Simmons Point, Balmain, in the 1890s, the wealthy occupy the high ground, where views and summer breezes are available.
MITCHELL LIBRARY

The tradesman who spent his day in vigorous employment could reap considerable rewards, including membership of the expanding middle class:

Even the less pretentious structures bear many marks of good taste, and an advanced order of embellishment. Indeed, the suburban villas of Sydney inhabited by the well-to-do tradesmen, the highly intelligent, quick-witted, practical, money-making middle classes, give one a high opinion of the material prosperity, and the solid domestic comfort which their appearance implies.[3]

Even a carpenter's standard of living was far above that of his English counterpart:

Here there is no drawing-room, but the parlour aspires to comfort quite undreamt of by an English tradesman. Our old friends the horse-hair cedar couch, the gent's and lady's chairs together with four balloon high chairs, turn up again. There is a four-foot chiffonier, a tapestry carpet, a gilt chimney-glass, a hearthrug, a bronze fender and fire-irons, and a round table with turned pillar and carved claws. In the parents' bedroom are a half-tester bedstead with coir-fibre or woollen flock mattress, two cane chairs, washstand, toilet-table, glass and ware, towel-horse, chest of drawers, and a couple of yards of bedside carpet. The two youngest children sleep in this room, and three or four others in the second bedroom, where the bedsteads are less showy and the ware very inferior. The carpet is replaced by china matting. The chest of drawers does duty as a toilet-table, and there are of course no such luxuries as towel-horses.[4]

Another luxury many builders did without was the advice of a qualified architect. Dismissing this

The interior of Grace-mere, the Archer family home at Rockhampton, Qld. The homestead was built of ironbark slabs in 1858; this photograph was taken during the 1880s.
JOHN OXLEY LIBRARY

Above: cane chairs and tables were extremely popular in Queensland, often crafted into a variety of shapes which managed to achieve a true Victorian clutter while keeping their occupants cool.
JOHN OXLEY LIBRARY

Right: 'A Hot Day in Town', from the *Australasian Sketcher* of 1899, catalogues the hammocks, cane furniture, plants and Chinese lanterns that were essential parts of the verandah lifestyle.

Above: the interior of Breffni reflects its owners' desire for the good life; a Persian rug, dozens of paintings and photographs on the plain walls, and a confusion of late Victorian bric-a-brac.
BATTYE LIBRARY

Left: more sedate, perhaps, than the owners of Breffni, Mr and Mrs Phillips relax in the comfortable drawing room of Culham at Toodyay, also in WA, in 1893.
BATTYE LIBRARY

One side of the fence is
sandy scrub; past the
white-painted gate lies
'civilisation' in the shape
of Breffni, a neat turn-
of-the century cottage in
suburban Subiaco, WA.

as expensive and unnecessary, they turned to the many pattern books that were readily available, or to backyard operators like John Buncle:

I made drawings of all kinds of imaginary houses suited for the locality, and, having coloured them in the most elaborate style and framed them, I now, when I saw a victim, offered to supply him with elevation plan and specification for any kind of house shown him for two guineas . . . it paid me splendidly because I only gave him a tracing.[5]

Designed with such expertise, and their construction unsupervised by any building inspectors, the suburban houses of Melbourne and Sydney began to cover the newly subdivided paddocks and farms. Although many of these areas are now fashionable, at the time they were considered by some to be the domain of the vulgar and tasteless. Architect Howard Joseland was of the opinion that:

the bounds of art in building were overstepped in the craze to produce new wonders that would appeal to the tastes of those who had suddenly risen from humble life. Foremost among the caterers to this market were the jerry-builders, and out of their ranks rose the 'jerry-architect'. As an outcome we see hideous stretches of terraces and wildernesses of villas in painted brick and cement, decked up with meaningless ironwork and atrocious ornament . . . Before the introduction of the many cheap ornaments in the form of plaster castings, cast ironwork and sawmill patterns, architects had to depend upon much simpler and legitimate means to gain effect [instead] of a display of vulgar ingenuity and untutored ideas . . . Many houses of this type, although seen equally well from the back and often from the sides, have all the ornamentation expended upon the front as though passers-by were supposed to shut their eyes till directly in front of the building. Strange to say, this architectural chaos had such a sway, and got such a hold upon the people, that they seem to have adopted it as an Australian style, so much so that monstrosities of the kind are even now being

perpetrated, though fortunately no longer by those who take a leading position in our profession.[6]

Such elitist criticism went unnoticed by the masses. The inhabitants of these 'monstrosities', blissfully unaware of the architectural horror surrounding them, were indulging a passion for home ownership seldom seen elsewhere in the world — on credit. R.E.N. Twopeny claimed in 1883:

The colonist is very fond of living in his own house and on his own bit of ground, and building societies and the extensive mortgage system which prevails enable him easily to gratify this desire. I believe

Darlinghurst, Sydney, viewed from Victoria Street around 1890, had already begun the long slide from wealth and 'respectability' to an overcrowded, vice-ridden slum.
GARRAN'S PICTURESQUE ATLAS OF AUSTRALIA

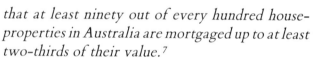

Above: thousands of cheap, identical and often jerry-built terraces were constructed in inner-city areas during the 1870s and 1880s to house an sharp increase in the number of immigrants.
MITCHELL LIBRARY

Above right: 'The squareness, or more properly the cubeness, of these two-storied houses is appalling,' wrote R.E.N. Twopeny of buildings such as this 1885 detached home in Melbourne (*Town Life in Australia*).
MUSEUM OF VICTORIA

that at least ninety out of every hundred house-properties in Australia are mortgaged up to at least two-thirds of their value.[7]

Twopeny went on to point out that beneath their 'unfortunate' exteriors, the new suburban houses concealed a chamber of structural horrors:

By far the majority of houses are built by speculators; which means that they are very badly built, run up in a tremendous hurry, constructed of the cheapest and nastiest materials, with thin walls — in short, built for show, and not for use. Everything looks very nice in them when you walk round just after they are built, and it is only after you have lived in them eighteen months that you begin to understand why the owner was in such a hurry to sell ...

In these speculative houses there is often some little attempt at ornamentation — a bow-window thrown out, or the veranda lifted to form a Gothic

porch, or the drawing-room brought out beyond the rest of the house, so as to form what is known as a T cottage, though it should rather be a P, with a protrusion of the drawing-room representing the straight line, and the body of the house the loop of the P.[8]

Some contemporary architects made full-scale attempts at ornamentation, with startling results. One critic, quoted in May 1887 in the Sydney *Builders and Contractors' News*, suggested some possible sources of inspiration:

Seeing the salt-cellar standing on the dining-table with the pepper-castor and the mustard pot on either side, he looks at them with the artist's eye, and at once evolves a new variety of castellated villa ... The villa architect takes a cathedral front and slices it up longitudinally; then an Elizabethan house, or a Chinese pagoda, a railway station, a hen-house, a dovecot, a pigsty — for art knows no

distinctions — and ... has an infinite number of phrases to work with and can vary the air to any extent ... The inside, like the meat in a penny pie, is generally an afterthought.

For those who wanted to develop original floor plans, Professor Kerr created an

ingenious device for shaking your ground-plan into shape. This consists simply in cutting out pieces of cardboard corresponding to the sizes of the required rooms, so that one card may represent the dining-room, another the library, another the breakfast parlour, and so on; and then bringing the separate pieces together, so as to group the whole into a convenient plan.[9]

Most commonly, however, the typical urban house plan was still the simple box:

The favourite type of Australian house is laid out in an oblong block bisected by a three to eight foot passage. The first door on one side as you go in is the drawing-room, on the other the dining-room. Then follow the bedrooms, etc., with the kitchen and scullery at the end of the passage, or sometimes in a lean-to at right angles to the hinder part of the house proper. This kind of cottage is almost universal in Adelaide amongst the middle and upper middle classes, and invariable in the working-class throughout Australia. In the other colonies the upper middle classes often live in two-storied houses; i.e., ground-floor and one floor above. Their construction is almost as simple as the cottage, the only difference being that the bedrooms are on the upper story, and that a pair of narrow stairs face the front-door and take up half the passage-way directly you get past the drawing and dining-room doors. The cottage is not high enough to strike the eye, but the squareness, or more properly the cubeness, of these two-storied houses is appalling. They look for all the world like

The middle class generally preferred uniformity in its suburban architecture, but occasionally free spirits like the Trevitt family (seen here in the 1880s outside their Chatswood, Sydney, home) broke free of convention — if only in minor ways, such as attic rooms.
NATIONAL LIBRARY OF AUSTRALIA

Scrupulously clean, the kitchen of this selector's slab house has been decorated with a valance neatly cut from newspaper.
CHARLES KERRY,
POWERHOUSE MUSEUM

houses built of cards, except that the cards are uncommonly solid. [10]

The kitchens were 'terribly small and in summer filled with flies', but:

Happily every house has a bath-room, though it is often only a mere shed of wood or galvanized iron put up in the back-yard. In many of the poorer households this shed does double duty as bath-house and wash-house, or the wash-house consists of a couple of boards, with a post to keep them up, and a piece of netting overhead to keep the sun off … Of the sanitary arrangements, it is almost impossible to speak too strongly; they are almost invariably objectionable and disgusting. [11]

One of the newest developments in the latter field was the earth closet, a device in which dry earth, clay, whiting, or ash was sprinkled into the pan after use to help absorb and deodorise the contents. In outer suburban areas, a deep pit was often employed.

In other cases, where the excavation was not of great depth, the privy had to be built on a square base into which the uprights were mortised so that it could be slid on skids to a new site when necessary. This lack of anchorage rendered them particularly vulnerable to the New Year's Eve pranks of the local 'talent'. The householder sometimes awoke to find this essential outhouse at his front gate, or reclining on its side. The site, of necessity a short distance away from the dwelling, was often fixed near the woodheap so that the return journey could provide for back-loading for the kitchen fire. [12]

With a plentiful and reliable water supply, however, public sewerage systems were created to service the inner suburbs of most cities, and water flushing closets, such as those of the tireless Yorkshire inventor Thomas Crapper, began to make their appearance.

Not to be outdone, Australians contributed their share of ideas for improving the quality of housing. One was the cavity brick wall. This innovation seems to have appeared around 1883, when some Australian builders began

encasing their brick buildings with a non-structural brick skin, leaving a gap of a couple of inches and tying the two leaves together with cast iron ties laid in alternate courses and staggered. The system meant that the porosity of the bricks and the mortar, which had been the main cause of trouble,

was no longer of much consequence. The outer leaf could become saturated with rain and water could run down its inner face but the inner structural wall remained dry and unaffected. It was used tentatively at first but within a few years its perfection was acknowledged. By 1895, when all buildings were brick, the cavity wall was standard practice. And from Australia it spread to the rest of the world — a genuine Australian contribution to world building practice.[13]

Also original were the metal ceilings of Ernest Wunderlich. In 1890 Wunderlich began to manufacture pressed zinc sheets for ceilings in an enormous range of popular designs. They were attractive, durable, fireproof and easy to install — a combination that guaranteed instant success. Inventions of all sorts began to invade the home

Above left: nightsoil carters might have queried claims that the earth closets of last century were odourless or handsome, but at least these 'conveniences' were mercifully warranted not liable to 'derangement'.

Above right: the invention of the water closet provided more than improvements in public health. Tireless artisans melded Art and Science in hygienic masterpieces such as this vitreous dolphin.

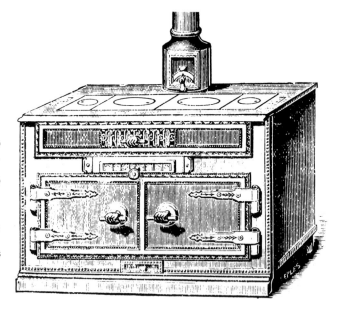

during the latter part of the nineteenth century. Almost everything was 'New and Improved' — washing machines, stoves, irons, bedsprings and water heaters. The rubber hose made gardening a simple business, and with the new hand-pushed 'amateur's' lawn-mower, a large expanse of buffalo-grass lawn could be kept under control, in conformity with developing suburban traditions.

Changes of a less savoury nature were taking place in many inner-city areas. As it became fashionable to live in the suburbs, with their clean air, fresh greenery and larger blocks of land, most who could afford to move did so. The space vacated by the middle class was filled by poorer families struggling to make ends meet. In order to pay the rent, as many people as possible crowded into these older houses, and the inadequate and often substandard water and drainage systems could not cope. Gradually the neighbourhood began to decline into 'a congerie of bare brick habitations … an arid desolate waste … utterly unrelieved by tree or grass'. Life became a precarious struggle for survival.

Out in the new suburbs, it was more of a struggle to be modern. Fashion magazines showed the way, while the avant-garde *Bulletin* promoted a new style of literature, art and nationalism — a self-assured 'Australian' confidence which was shaken suddenly by events in the outside world. A financial crash in Argentina created problems for the English banks, causing them in turn to recall their capital from Australia. Without this support, vast numbers of artificially prosperous banks, building societies and self-assured companies collapsed, taking with them the fortunes of investors large and small. The booming building industry came to a sudden halt and hundreds of thousands were thrown out of work. Suddenly even the rich were poor.

The resulting depression made life in the slums even more unbearable, causing some adventurous optimists to forsake the poverty of the city in favour of the wide open spaces. They found to their disappointment that things there were not much better.

To finance their land purchases in the 1850s and 1860s, and the improvement and expansion of their properties during the 1870s and 1880s, many squatters went heavily into debt. Then, unexpectedly, prices began to fall and long periods of drought forced many pastoralists into bankruptcy. Unwise investment in suburban land speculation and similar schemes sent others to the wall when the crash came; their properties were sold up by the banks and their helpful friends, the stock and station agents.

Those who survived often occupied homes with much more style and comfort than they had previously enjoyed:

The homestead itself is a substantial house of stone, built after the fashion of a bungalow, with only one storey, and a broad verandah running around three sides of it. Grape-vines and passion-flower shade the verandah, and the front of the house looks over a spacious garden and orchard, with a thick hedge of quince trees. On the verandah are easy chairs and lounges, and a table strewn with the latest English magazines, as well as the admirable weekly papers that are a feature of Australian journalism. The windows run down to the floor; the doorway is wide and inviting, and opens to a spacious cool-tiled hall. On one side is a drawing-room, with grand piano, polished floors, and Persian rugs; water-colours are on the walls and large mirrors, all in the best modern taste. On the other side is a dining-room, large and handsomely furnished, and behind it a cheerful morning-room; with the newest novels lining the bookshelf, and the latest music on the upright piano. Bedrooms, cool and airy, open onto the wide verandah, but to see the kitchen and laundry it is necessary to pass to a group of detached buildings in the rear.[14]

Superficially, the selector began life on the land in conditions almost identical to those of the squatter — but the similarity ended there. The selectors, on small blocks and with very limited financial resources, found it difficult enough to be self-sufficient let alone make profits that would finance improvements.

A conditional purchaser's simple slab hut, with the tools with which he hoped to secure permanent title ready for the arduous labour of clearing and fencing what was often rough country.

Steele Rudd and Henry Lawson were both familiar with the plight of the selector, trapped in a web of poverty. The following description by Henry Lawson of a selector's hut is not markedly different from that of Big Mick's habitation as recorded in *Ralph Rashleigh* some seventy years earlier:

The hut was nearly as bare inside as it was out — just a frame of 'round-timber' (sapling poles) covered with bark. The furniture was permanent (unless you rooted it up), like in our kitchen: a rough slab table on stakes driven into the ground, and seats made the same way. Mary told me

afterwards that the beds in the bag-and-bark partitioned-off room ('mother's bedroom') were simply poles laid side by side on cross-pieces supported by stakes driven into the ground, with straw mattresses and some worn-out bed-clothes. Mrs Spicer had an old patchwork quilt, in rags, and the remains of a white one, and Mary said it was pitiful to see how these things would be spread over the beds — to hide them as much as possible — when she went down there. A packing-case, with something like an old print skirt draped round it, and a cracked looking-glass (without a frame) on top, was the dressing-table. There were a couple of gin-cases for a wardrobe. The boys' beds

Above: stump-jump ploughs and Sunshine harvesters notwithstanding, success in farming meant intensive labour — usually provided free by an apparently endless number of children.
GIPPSLAND HISTORICAL SOCIETY

Left: this corrugated-iron miner's hut on the Coolgardie, WA, goldfields would have been unbearably hot but for the brush wired to the posts to provide a primitive but fairly effective form of insulation.
BATTYE LIBRARY

Above: West Australian selector Jack Nicholas built this neat home for his wife and daughter Margaretta in the 1890s.
BATTYE LIBRARY

Right: Mr and Mrs A. McWatters face the photographer and the coming of the new century in poses of mingled resignation and hope, from the steps of their New England, NSW, cottage in the last days of the 1890s.
NEW ENGLAND HISTORICAL RESOURCES CENTRE

were three-bushel bags stretched between poles fastened to uprights. The floor was the original surface, tramped hard, worn uneven with much sweeping, and with puddles in rainy weather where the roof leaked. Mrs Spicer used to stand old tins, dishes, and buckets under as many of the leaks as she could. The sauce-pans, kettles and boilers were old kerosene-tins and billies.[15]

Yet the dreamers, the immigrants and the optimists continued to take up where others had left:

You'll ride all over it filled with the proud spirit of ownership. Every inch of it and everything on it will be yours — the growing timber; the logs and firewood lying about; hundreds of fencing-posts that some poor cove's split and had to abandon; the old sheepyard and shepherd's hut that were erected by someone who went insolvent; even the wild flowers and darn stones 'll be yours! How you'll admire it all![16]

Bert Facey, in *A Fortunate Life*, describes how his family built their first bush home in 1895:

Uncle Archie and my brothers were busy building a house. I suppose it would be called a humpy. They cut the poles about twelve feet long, and six inches thick at one end and about three to four inches thick at the other. They cut hundreds of them and carted them to where they intended to build the humpy ... Then Uncle and the boys dug a trench at each end and put poles in them in the same way, joining the two fifty foot walls together. Then they put up two dividing walls, making a twelve by twelve room at each end of the structure and leaving a living and dining-room in the centre, twenty-six feet by twelve. They then put a roof over the three rooms and thatched it with blackboy spines ...

Uncle Archie and Aunt Alice had one of the twelve-foot rooms for their bedroom and Grandma and the girls the other. We boys slept in tents outside. Uncle made a door frame for the big room out of bush timber, and sewed kangaroo skins on to it to keep out the cold weather and water. The doorways leading into the bedrooms had only

Above: building a homestead in the 1890s. No doubt, the owner can already see its 'large and handsomely furnished [rooms] ... with the newest novels lining the bookshelf, and the latest music on the upright piano'.
BATTYE LIBRARY

Left: corrugated iron was invented in 1829, galvanising in 1837. The first galvanised iron was imported into Australia in the 1840s ... and we have been infatuated by it ever since.

curtains over them. When the building and thatching were finished, Uncle and the boys dug out clay from the creek which ran through the property, and after making it very wet and soft, they pushed it into the cracks of the poles that made the walls. When it was dry it made the place nice and weather-proof.[17]

Building even a simple house oneself was not always as easy as the experts suggested. E.J. Banfield moved to Dunk Island on the Barrier

Brick and corrugated iron were expensive, manufactured items and had to wait for a comfortable bank balance. Wood, especially in Tasmania, was cheap and was employed liberally.

Reef in search of an existence 'nearer to nature, and though the advantages of civilisation remain unforfeited, to the happy condition of the simple uncomplicated man'. Complications arose, however, when he began building:

According to the formula neatly printed in official journals, the building of a slab hut is absurdly easy — quite a pastime for the settler eager to get a roof of bark or thatch over his head. The frame, of course, goes up without assistance, and then the principal item is the slabs for walls. When you have fallen your tree and sawn off a block of the

required length, you have only to split off the slab. Ah! but suppose the timber does not split freely, and your heavy maul does; and the wedges instead of entering have the habit of bouncing out as if they were fitted with internal springs, and your maul wants renewal several times, until you find that the timber prescribed is of no account for such tools; and at best your slabs run off to nothing at half length, and several trees have to be cut down before you get a single decent slab, and everybody is peevish with weariness and disappointment, the rudest house in the bush will be a long time in the building. 'Experience is a hard mistress, yet she

Above: economic problems in both city and country meant many settlers' dreams had to be modified. This Victorian selector is no doubt waiting for better times before adding a verandah to his cottage.
MUSEUM OF VICTORIA

Left: thrift and caution are rural virtues exemplified by the South Australian 'backender' a skillion-roofed, stone-house which would become the rear of a substantial homestead if prosperity arrived. If didn't, the owners merely added a porch and continued to occupy their odd-looking but comfortable home.
STATE LIBRARY OF SA

129

Edward Sorenson noted that a hollow tree-stump makes 'a capital first residence'; some eccentrics, however, elected to remain in these unusual — if rather cramped —quarters.
GIPPSLAND HISTORICAL SOCIETY

teacheth as none other.' We came to be more indebted to the hard mistress — she gave us blistering palms and aching muscles — than to all the directions and prescriptions of men who claim to have climbed to the top of the tree in the profession of the 'bush'. A 'bush' carpenter is a very admirable person, when he is not also a bush lawyer. Mere amateurs would be wise if they held their enthusiasm in check when they read the recipe — pat as the recipe for the making of a rice-pudding — for the construction of even a bark hut. It is so very easy to write it all down; but if you have had no actual experience in bark-cutting, and your trees are not in the right condition, you will put your elation to a shockingly severe test, harden the epidermis of your hands, and the whole of your heart, and go to bed many nights sadly ere you get one decent sheet for your roof.[18]

Some pioneers decided that a more logical course of action was simply to occupy the tree. Several of these tree-houses were noticed by Edward Sorenson, author of *Life in the Australian Backblocks*:

The crudest habitations are found among the giant timber of Gippsland. The upper part of a big hollow tree is sawn off, and a roof put on. Sometimes the top is left intact, and there may be two or three floors built inside the trunk, with little windows cut out here and there. This tree-house makes a capital first residence, and may afterwards be turned into a kitchen, stable, store or poultry-house. It is more roomy than a stranger might suppose. Commissary Hall, who lived at O'Brien's Bridge, Hobart, recorded of a tree on his property: 'It is a trifle over 300 feet, and there are some fifty feet of the top blown off. I myself have seen fourteen men on horseback in the hollow of it. In 1854 Sir William Denison, the Governor, and seventy-eight of the Legislative Assembly and their friends, dined in the hollow of it.'[19]

Another house at Tomki, on the Richmond River, was built on four living stumps sawn off 2.5 metres above the ground. The stumps had sprouted, covering the whole house with greenery.

Often stumps were all that remained of the once densely forested bush, since selectors believed it was necessary to clear-fell to increase productivity. Even useful trees such as the stringybark were destroyed. In 'The Stringy-Bark Tree,' a poem written around the turn of the century, Lawson mourned its comparative scarcity:

There's the whitebox and pine on the ridges afar,
Where the iron-bark, blue gum and peppermint are,
There is many another but dearest to me,
And the king of them all is the stringy-bark tree.

Then of stringy-bark slabs were the walls of the hut,
And from stringy-bark saplings the rafters were cut;
And the roof that long sheltered my brothers and me
Was broad sheets of bark from the stringy-bark tree.

Far up the long gullies the timber-trucks went
Over tracks that seemed hopeless, by bark hut and tent;
And the gaunt timber finder who rode at his ease,
Led them on to a gully of stringy-bark trees.

Now still from the ridges by ways that are dark,
Come the shingles and palings they call stringy-bark;
Though you ride through long gullies a twelve-month
you'll see
But the old whitened stumps of the stringy-bark tree.

In some areas the mobile home proved a popular choice:

In and around Broken Hill many people live in houses built on wheels, and it is common to see cottages travelling about, leaving gaps in one street and filling vacancies in another. Removing in the Silver City means taking the house with you. They are sometimes drawn up to the auction-mart and sold. I saw only one selector in a habitation of this kind. He had been a travelling saddler and cobbler, and when he selected he simply drew his saddle and harness shop into position and settled down.[20]

Mud-brick and pisé houses were now particularly favoured in western New South Wales and in Queensland, where other building materials were in short supply. Bertie Rayment, a pioneer of the Windorah district in Queensland, gave the following recipe for construction:

Depression or not, the early 1890s saw a tremendous influx of migrants eager to build a new life in a new land. These Italian settlers have almost completed a mud-brick home in northwestern Victoria. MUSEUM OF VICTORIA

A fairly solid foundation is prepared. The mud, as near real red clay as possible, must be thoroughly mixed, but no straw is required. Layers of about one foot are placed all around the building and wet bagging is used to keep it from drying too quickly until another layer can be put on. Wood is used only in windows and door frames and wall plates. When the wall is up, it is levelled off and gone over with a wet rag as if for scrubbing. It is let dry for a few days, depending on the time of the year (in winter as long as a week). The next step is important. Soak boiling or near boiling fat or a paint oil as far into the mud as possible. In the back country beef fat is usually used because linseed oil has always been costly.

The best way to do this, especially in winter, is to light a fire as big as possible in each room before the roof is put on, making use of the heat of the sun, the idea being to get the fairly dry mud wall hot while the heat is in the wall. Put as much boiling oil as the wall will absorb; use a swab. If the oil penetrates three-quarters of an inch into the mud inside and out, the wall will be a good one. The rest of the work is for the ordinary carpenter.[21]

Sorenson also remarked on the use of fat in these buildings:

Similar structures are still in use west of Windorah, the walls built of earth and tallow, and the floors of ashes and tallow, which set like cement. Currawilla Station, in this neighbourhood, is surrounded by a great wall, eight feet high, built of the same material. The enclosure prevents the homestead being inundated when the flood comes down Farrar's Creek. It is a unique sight to see this place low and dry in the midst of miles of seething waters. The blending of tallow makes the walls waterproof, and also prevents erosion when subjected to a strong current.[22]

Many inhabitants of low-lying areas in Brisbane would have been grateful for similar protection as

Away from the public eye, the suburban backyard was the real focus of family life. With their dogs and pet cockatoo for company, this family is preparing homemade sausages to a recipe probably brought with them to Australia.
MUSEUM OF VICTORIA

Not even the high-set Queenslanders were protected from the devastating floods that hit Brisbane in 1893. Many poorly built houses simply disappeared in the swirling waters.
JOHN OXLEY LIBRARY

the massive floods of 1893 rose around them, causing much damage and chaos.

Even more frightening were cyclones such as the one that struck Darwin in 1897. Many houses could not withstand the incredible gale-force winds which blew for several hours, leaving the city almost totally wrecked. Dudley Kelsey, a telegraphist for the Overland Telegraph, was at work during the storm. When it was over he hurried out to find his wife and son safe, but:

Our home of four rooms, with 12 ft. front, east side and back verandahs, was in ruins. The four rooms and front verandah were built on piles, and the east and back verandah were on stone, cemented over. The two back rooms had moved eleven feet back; the two front rooms and the verandah had collapsed altogether, and the whole of the roofing was missing.

With the assistance of a black boy I got to work, and was soon able to have my wife and child more comfortably quartered. Luckily, the kitchen at the rear of the house was in a more sheltered position, and was still standing. Breaking up some of the

fittings for firewood, I soon had a fire going and some hot coffee ready. Then I tried to find some dry clothing for my wife and little son. They were almost perishing with cold after their long night out in the rain.

When they were settled, I busied myself and soon had some roofing back on the house. By evening the boy and I had the two back rooms habitable, although the furniture and bed clothes were still wet. It rained all day, and clothes had to be dried in front of the kitchen fire. The furniture of the two front rooms was in a heap, damaged greatly by fallen timber, and rain. Strangely, a small glass specimen case containing about twenty-eight pounds of minerals, was found lying on its side without even the glass broken. Our piano was soaked, but a few days later we were able to play it to cheer our spirits.[23]

Just as the Kelseys sang around their soggy piano, so the rest of the nation began to recover from the disasters of the 1890s and look forward with renewed optimism to the unknown possiblities of the twentieth century.

Left: cool and shaded in summer, and protected from the winter winds, in Australian country houses the verandah became more of an outdoor room than a mere shelter.
FRYER LIBRARY

Above: despite the booms and depressions that saw many squatters forced off their properties, station life could be pleasant and peaceful — especially during a musical evening.
BATTYE LIBRARY

'Distinctively Australian' 1900-1920

ON 1 JANUARY 1901, IN EXCHANGE FOR A PLEDGE OF undying loyalty to Queen Victoria, Her Majesty's government bestowed on Australia the status of an independent nation. In an orgy of patriotic fervour, Australians responded by painting the town red — literally. A new Federation architecture of red-brick houses with orange-tiled roofs began to infiltrate the suburbs of Sydney and Melbourne. These Edwardian houses were the product of a combination of ideas, materials and designs.

The first was the need to develop some 'distinctively Australian order of architecture', as artist Lucien Henry put it. He suggested that this could be achieved simply enough: 'by the application to it of designs and colours borrowed from our indigenous fauna and flora, selecting for treatment ... the lyre bird and the Tasmanian hippocampus, and the waratah, the stenocarpus, the protea, the actinotus, the stag's horn fern, the mangrove, the screw-palm, and the gigantic lily of Queensland.'[1] Aboriginal heads were also considered suitable indigenous decorative motifs; a nice sense of irony in a country in search of its identity.

Many of these decorations found their way on to the roofs and gable ends of houses, where they were combined with the bright orange terracotta Marseilles tiles that had first appeared in Australia in 1886. Ernest Wunderlich was quick to see the potential of this form of roofing and, backed by a solid advertising campaign, began importing large quantities from France. By 1914 enough tiles to roof 40 000 homes had passed through the company's hands.

Shipments ceased at the outbreak of World War I, but, unwilling to see an Australia so deprived, Wunderlich opened his own factories producing, in addition to tiles, accessories such as kookaburra and kangaroo finials as an alternative to the more flamboyant European dragons and gryphons.

Fashion aside, roof tiles were a sensible alternative to slate and galvanised iron. The many chinks between them allowed some ventilation of the roof space and their thickness created cooler conditions inside the house. No one could have summed up their advantages better than Wunderlich; indeed, no one had as much incentive to do so:

The artistic trend of domestic architecture gives the architect great scope for picturesque outlines in his designs, and the quaint gables, chimney stacks and skyline of the modern home is greatly enhanced by the use of terracotta roofing tiles and accessories. There is a restful charm about the villa roofed with Wunderlich Marseilles tiles. The deep shadows of its overhanging eaves and gables breathe that feeling of repose only assured under a roof which is sound and weather proof.

Marseilles tiles ... are rich in colour, strong, reliable, of hard surface, absorption of moisture reduced to a minimum, and they are perfect insulators and keep the building warm in Winter

Facing page
Symbol, perhaps, of the bright hope brought by the new century, the rising sun remained a popular motif in Australian houses until the 1930s; it was employed both externally and for interior details.
MUSEUM OF VICTORIA

137

Above: outside the cities fashions were slow to affect architectural style; Fernhem, at Sassafras in the Dandenong Ranges north of Melbourne, was a simple, self-contained mountain home.
LATROBE LIBRARY

Right: the Federation style was far more sober in Queensland, where decoration was largely restricted to window-hood detailing and turned or fretted woodwork around the verandah.
JOHN OXLEY LIBRARY

and cool in Summer. The ideal roof for the country.

Marseilles tiles are clean and cool; rain water from a tile roof is sweet and pure. Proof against fire or hail storms. Our tiles are imperishable and withstand climatic changes.[2]

Red bricks were the next ingredient. Previously, paler bricks in cream and buff had been popular — and, in any case, clays from different areas naturally produced bricks of varying shades. Now, however, red clay was especially sought, or attempts were made to colour the pug artificially before firing so a uniformly red brick would result.

The now common cavity wall allowed houses to expose more raw brick wall to the weather without fear of internal damp. This brickwork was often highlighted by tuck-pointing, giving the walls a crisp and neat appearance.

In Victoria, 'indigenous' decoration, tile, and red brick were frequently combined with an imported architectural style known as 'Queen Anne'. Made popular by the English architect Richard Norman Shaw, the Queen Anne style was in fact inspired by houses built during the reign of Queen Elizabeth I. Its most obvious characteristic was its 'picturesque' steeply pitched, multi-faceted roof, with spires, dormers and false gables, the ridges trimmed with a frilly edge of patterned terracotta.

Sometimes long rectangular banks of leadlight casement windows replaced the heavy counter-weighted, double-hung sashes of the Victorian era. Queen Anne front doors often featured coloured leadlight panels in the style of Art Nouveau, as well as ornate brass knockers and doorbells.

Other capital cities produced their own variations on Federation architecture, and at the same time some architects began to show an interest in small houses as well as mansions. Probably the

Fashion did not always equate with beauty: the boxy design of this Perth cottage is hardly attractive, and its mass of red brick and narrow eaves are unsuited to the West Australian climate.
BATTYE LIBRARY

139

The relentless spread of suburbia can be traced by the evolution of building styles. Photographed in 1911 these cottages, in the Fernhill Estate, Sydney, represent the first flush of the Federation style.

most visionary of these was Robert Haddon, author of *Australian Architecture*, who wrote in 1908:

It is with the suburban villa that the greatest house-building activity will always prevail, and there good work and bad will the most commingle with the sway of popular taste, and the come and go of styles, mannerisms, and modes of life.

That in suburban house building there is great opportunity of reform, as there is also equal opportunity to do good work, there can be no doubt.[3]

Real-estate entrepreneur Richard Stanton had no doubts at all when in 1901 he created the garden suburb of Haberfield, 'within 32 minutes from the General Post Office, Sydney, by electric tram'. House and land were sold as a package, with each cottage architect-designed to the individual customer's budget and requirements. Haberfield was promoted as 'the place of beautiful homes'. A building covenant stated: 'only double fronted brick cottages permitted to a value of at least £400. Weatherboard and inferior residences absolutely excluded ... [with] every view a delight fronting wide avenues of shade trees.'

Following Stanton's success, the New South Wales government attempted a similar public housing project at Dacey Gardens, to show that it was 'making an effort to create an Australian model in providing homes for the people in the shape of a garden city'. Unfortunately there was more political rhetoric and high idealism than money — a common situation in public housing — and only a fraction of the houses proposed were ever built.

Above: Federation style in a modest Sydney villa: red Marseilles tiles, tuck-pointed brickwork, casement windows, ornamental entry porch woodwork, and cement-rendered half timbering.

Left: rigid conventions of manners and style eased following Victoria's death, and the Edwardians' delighted rediscovery of Nature found expression in curvilinear forms, inside *and* out.
JOHN OXLEY LIBRARY

141

Above: Sydney's Rocks district (now, as at the turn of the century, a museum of architectural development in Australia) received a much-needed spring cleaning in 1901, when an outbreak of bubonic plague was traced to its vermin-infested hovels.
ROBERT PRICE COLLECTION

Right: a row of efficient, if characterless, worker's cottages designed by architect Cyril Blackett and located hard by the railway line at Thornleigh, on Sydney's North Shore.
MITCHELL LIBRARY

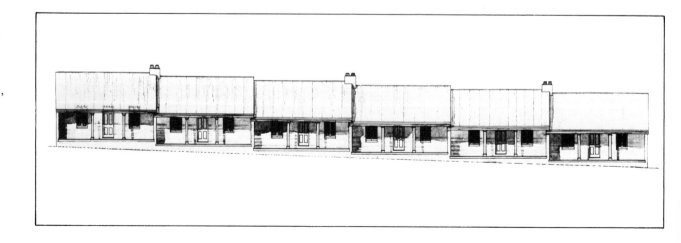

Harold Cazneaux's 1911 photograph of urchins at play in a Surry Hills street has its charm, but conveys little about conditions in the inner-Sydney slum area.

One of the few descriptions of suburbia in the
early 1900s was recorded by an English visitor,
E.C. Buley, in 1905:

*Here the houses are all single-storied bungalows,
or villas, as the Australians prefer to call them,
each standing in its own plot of garden. Glance
over the fragrant pittosporum hedge, and you may
see the lawn sprinkler pleasantly at work upon a
grass plot bordered with masses of bright phlox
and thriving roses and pelargoniums . . . There is an
air of roominess and privacy about these Australian suburbs that stands for a good deal of solid
comfort. The citizen swings in his hammock and
smokes his pipe without any consciousness of being
observed from the top floor of some building close
at hand . . . The most arduous task of the amateur
gardener is the constant use of the watering-can;
the rest is done by Nature with a lavish hand. The*
*vine and the fig tree are by no means impossible,
and a rough erection of wooden laths makes an
ideal fern-house.*

*These things figure very largely in the life of the
average Australian city-dweller, who leaves his
city office at five, changes into easy clothing as
soon as he arrives home, dines comfortably about
half-past six, and then potters about his garden
until it grows dark.* [4]

Some city dwellers had no gardens to potter
about in. Terraces were still being built with a
narrow strip of ground in front and a small dark
yard at the rear. Architect J.S. Gawler recalls the
houses in a typical middle-class Melbourne suburb
around the turn of the century:

*Many of the terraces had cemented gables or
parapets over the front wall facing the street with*

A busy corner of the sitting room at Strathallan, the Gundagai home of the Bruce family, around 1900. Next to the screened *faux marbre* fireplace is a Perfection oil heater.
NATIONAL LIBRARY OF AUSTRALIA

pressed cement ornament and raised cement letters giving a name to each house. These names always amused me; they ranged from castles on the Rhine, names of girls, racehorses or characters from classical mythology. Enter the front door and you are in a narrow ill lit passage dignified by the name of 'hall' from a remote ancestry of the baronial halls of England. Should you be a visitor, the parson or the doctor, you would be shown into the front room, the drawing room, the holy of holies where many families kept a small museum. The best room in the house, it was used the least, but contained the costliest furniture; various jimcrack tables, a piano, and the mantelpiece were covered with a collection of family photos and other curios; sometimes the parents' wedding photo enlargement hung over the mantelpiece and dad was wearing white gloves! An old fashioned venetian blind and some heavy curtains kept the light dim, saving the antimacassars from fading and the aspidestra from growing. Mother entertained her lady friends in this room if they were important

enough, but the children rarely entered for fear they might damage something, in fact I remember one house I visited where the door was locked to keep them out.

Next was the dining room dedicated to Sunday dinner and other important family meals. It couldn't be used for everyday meals because of carrying everything from the kitchen. A large table and stiff chairs took up a big part of the room, a heavy sideboard and a projecting brick fireplace, possibly a sofa, used up much of the remaining space. There was a cast iron grate with a row of ugly tiles each side, a heavy mantel with an overmantel generally with a number of small bevelled mirrors in fancy shapes with a few small shelves here and there. Mother and father would sit there in the evening while the children did their home lessons in the kitchen.

The kitchen was behind the dining room, but not connected to it directly; it often had a lean-to roof and a not very ample window. A one fire stove in a brick fireplace was in the darkest corner. The mother of the family was lucky if the kitchen didn't catch the hot afternoon sun in summer. In this room the family lived and flourished from hurried morning breakfast to late dinner when father came home from work. In its badly lit and cheerless environment the wife and mother spent much of her time and naturally got 'fed up' now and then. Often there was a further room, the scullery, behind the kitchen containing a black iron sink in the darkest corner, sometimes also a bricked in copper and a mangle. Many homes had no scullery and no sink at all, nor any copper.

The bedrooms often faced a fence only a few feet away or the wall of the next house, rarely painted or clean. I can remember living in such a house in Carlton and listening with boyish interest to the people in the next house quarrelling. Many of these bedrooms never got a gleam of sunlight, summer or winter. The bathroom, if there was one, was a narrow crack of a room, with a very small window or skylight and had a sheet iron bath, a fuel hot water heater, and generally a small basin, not always with even a cold water.[5]

Above: the dining room at Strathallan is obviously the turn-of-the century equivalent of a 'family room'. The acetylene-fuelled lamp above the table was designed by Ernest Bruce.
NATIONAL LIBRARY OF AUSTRALIA

Left: in this rare photograph of the interior of a Darlinghurst terrace, Harold Cazneaux (right) operated his Midge box camera by remote control (a length of cotton thread) to take 'Visitor From Town' in 1906.

The floor covering in such houses was often linoleum, invented in England by Frederick Walton in 1860. In his memoirs he wrote that he 'made up the coined word from *linum*, flax, and *oleum*, oil; that is linseed oil — the basis of the cement'.[6]

Printed with brightly coloured patterns (sometimes duplicating timber, marble or Persian rugs), cheap, durable, and easy to clean, linoleum became a favourite choice in many homes. Naturally this involved catering to a wide variety of tastes. One dissertation in 1905 suggested that there should be three sorts of designs:

designs that are good floor covering, pleasing in form, and harmonious in the theory of design, to suit the public that is educated and knows what a design should be;

where elaborate floral devices in bunches or strewn in garlands form the principal theme in loud and contrasting colours, that a certain number of uneducated people can best get their money's worth in noise and brilliancy;

and a class of design for the great middle class that knows these florid and ostentatious designs are in bad taste; but that does not feel itself equal to the appreciation of the first lot and therefore must be content with simple, inoffensive patterns, whose main virtues lie in the fact that even though one cannot say they are good, he cannot say they are very bad.[7]

One of the taste-makers of the day insisted that an atmosphere of 'artistic charm' could only be achieved by having walls of palest hues. But it could not be allowed to stop there: 'Remember always,' she cautioned the unwary,

that walls are but backgrounds to things and people, and that light walls, with old-fashioned furniture, are the acme of bad taste, so that to keep hopelessly ugly carpets, curtains, and furniture is only the means of spoiling your artistic eye, and of preventing both brightness and charm to surround you. It is far better to get rid of them at once, and replace them by simple up-to-date items.[8]

In a 1906 volume of the *Tribune*, a wag satirised this transition from Victorian to Edwardian taste in his poem, 'Peaceful Furniture':

He lived in a riot of painting,
Of carpets that screamed their surprise.
His guests were oft carried out fainting
Through the strength of the wallpaper's cries.

His curtains were rowdy and blatant,
His mats had a hooligan air;
His chairs, it was brutally patent,
Were designed for the raising of hair.

From couches came horrible moaning,
Occasional tables ran mad.
And ever the sideboard kept groaning
In a way that was bitterly bad.

His beated brain seethed like a crater;
He anguished for quiet and peace.
Till he called in a Skilled Decorator,
Who said, 'All the tumult shall cease:

'Your pictures must be without colour,
Your curtains resemble a pall,
The scheme of your carpets grow duller —
In fact, why a carpet at all?

'I shall strip your wallpaper of passion,
In its place you shall have neutral grey;
An arctic frieze quite in fashion
Shall solace your eyes night and day.

'As to sideboard, chairs, couches, and tables,
And objects that litter your floor,
Consign them to outhouse or stables
And list to their ravings no more.'

The householder dumbly assented,
And now he's as merry as May.
For he sits at his ease, undemented,
In a solitude vasty and grey.

In the cultural wilderness of the Northern Territory Jeannie Gunn was confronted by another original form of wall decoration when she arrived to take up residence at Elsey Station:

As for the walls, not only were the 'works of art' there, but they themselves were uniquely dotted

from ceiling to floor with the muddy imprints of dogs' feet — not left there by a Pegasus breed of winged dogs, but made by the muddy feet of the station dogs, as they pattered over the timber, when it lay awaiting the carpenter, and no one had seen any necessity to remove them.'⁹

Life in the 'last frontier' was too relaxed to take house building very seriously. The desert climate meant that shade and little else was a high priority. The original Elsey homestead had been wrecked by the cyclone of 1897 and was partly rebuilt by an itinerant Chinese carpenter, who was also responsible for the design:

His plans showed a wide-roofed building, built upon two-foot piles, with two large centre rooms opening into each other and surrounded by a deep verandah on every side; while two small rooms, a bathroom and an office, were to nestle each under one of the eastern corners of this deep twelve-foot verandah. Without a doubt, excellent common-sense ideas; but, unfortunately, much larger than the supply of timber. Rough-hewn posts for the two-foot piles and verandah supports could be had for the cutting, and therefore did not give out; but the man used joists and uprights with such reckless extravagance, that by the time the skeleton of the building was up, the completion of the contract was impossible. With philosophical indifference, however, he finished one room completely; left a second a mere outline of uprights and tye-beams; apparently forgot all about the bathroom and office; covered the whole roof, including verandahs, with corrugated iron; surveyed his work with a certain amount of stolid satisfaction; then announcing that 'wood bin finissem', applied for

'Old-fashioned furniture' might have been 'the acme of bad taste' in the era of Art Nouveau, but not every-one could throw away yesterday's style. Instead, they mixed new with old to create a distinctly uncomfortable melange.
BATTYE LIBRARY

Above: kerosene tins, and even the boxes in which tins were sold, were universally useful items. More than one hardy (if impoverished) settler relied on flattened 'kero' tins as a building material.
CHARLES KERRY, POWERHOUSE MUSEUM

Right: fresh from the Old Country, J.C. Gomme took up land at 'Bermia' near Bridgetown, WA, in 1905 and housed his family in a hut with walls of wheat bags and a galvanised-iron roof.
BATTYE LIBRARY

his cheque and departed; and from that day nothing further has been done to the House, which stood before us 'mostly verandahs and promises'.[10]

While the architects and interior decorators searched for a 'solution that was truly indigenous', country people simply built what they could. One of the enduring qualities of Australians is their ability to improvise. Photographs of the period show people living comfortably in 100000-litre water tanks. One house in Western Australia was even made from empty bully-beef tins laid like bricks in clay mortar, with a roof covered with shingles also made from flattened cans; others, in New South Wales and Victoria, had walls of flattened kerosene tins.

Dorothy Roysland, in *A Pioneer Family on the* *Murray River*, recalls that her family home near Renmark, South Australia, was made out of wheat bags; such rural houses were not uncommon:

This first home of ours was fairly primitive by today's standards. The walls of the rooms were all made of wheat-bags nailed to the wooden supports. We children had to cut through the twine stitching on these bags, give them a good shaking to get rid of any loose pieces, then lay them out lengthways and sew them together until we had an area big enough to cover one wall. When the entire wooden frame was covered, the iron roof was put on, and then we painted the walls with a mixture of lime and cement. This dried very hard, making the hessian firm and rigid. Next we made another mixture of lime and cement, but this time with

Tinned Dog Hut on the Norseman goldfields of Western Australia was built entirely of bully beef cans. Some walls, like the roof, were made of flattened cans; others were built of cans laid in mortar.
BATTYE LIBRARY

151

much less cement in it, and painted the walls again. When this second coating had dried the walls were a nice whitish colour.

The kitchen was a very long room, I remember, and it never had a proper door. One corner of uncemented bag wall was just left hanging so that we could push our way in or out. We never had any really good furniture. In the kitchen we had a large wooden table that we could all sit around, with two long green-painted wooden benches that went right down either side, and a couple of chairs, one at each end. We had an old kitchen dresser to hold our cups and saucers and plates, and another makeshift cupboard made from kerosene boxes. These boxes could be used in many ways. They made useful extra seats, and when five or six were laid on top of one another they made good shelves. Mother put a curtain around our kerosene-box kitchen cupboard and we kept all our cooking utensils and washing-up pans and big boilers in it . . .

Mother did the cooking on a colonial oven, the sort made of iron bars standing on bricks, with a fire in the top part. You could boil kettles and saucepans on top, but if you wanted to use the oven part you had to light a fire underneath. We also had a big camp oven, a huge flat-bottomed iron post standing on legs and covered with a heavy lid . . .

As well as the kitchen we had what we called our dining-room, but this was hardly ever used. Here there were an old-fashioned couch covered in green plush, two armchairs, and a three cornered cupboard pushed into one corner. My bed was in this room, and Mother's room adjoined. Mother had a large bed covered with a fringed honeycomb quilt. Next to this was a real dressing-table, with a mirror and drawers, and a big box couch in which our clothes were stored. She also had a homemade wardrobe — a triangular frame put into a corner, with a curtain hanging in front. Behind the curtain a few pieces of wood had been tacked up, and Mother hung her dresses from these on homemade coat-hangers.[11]

Dorothy continued by describing how she papered

the walls of the house as a surprise for her mother:

On another occasion when Mother was away I planned to paper the bag walls of our house. I brought out a pile of old newspapers and mixed up a bucketful of paste made from flour and water, and I was ready. When all the walls were covered I gave them time to dry out, and then I stirred up a mixture of water and red ochre to use as paint. I added a handful of flour so that it would stick to the paper and not rub off, and then I painted the colour all over the walls with a brush so that it covered up all the newsprint. It dried a lovely pink, and looked very fine. Mother was delighted with it.[12]

Another typical product of Australian ingenuity was the Coolgardie safe, a simple but effective cooling device employed in country homes until supplanted by the ice chest. Most were homemade, like that used by Dorothy's family:

We never knew what it was to have electricity laid on: I don't think it ever entered our minds. We were quite happy with our open fires and hurricane lamps. There were no washing-machines or refrigerators in our home. In summer our food was kept cool in a homemade Coolgardie safe made out of hessian bags. We kept the sides of the safe wet by filling a water container at the top and letting it overflow, and the evaporation of water from the hessian kept the inside of the safe nice and cool. There were no automatic water heaters, either. We always had open fires lit outside to boil up the kerosene tins of water we used for washing up the dishes and doing the weekly wash, and for our baths as well. We had no wash troughs, only tubs, and when we washed our clothes and linen we had to use wooden or tin washing-boards and big bars of homemade common soap. We bathed in these washtubs as well, for we had no proper bathroom.[13]

Although many houses did not yet contain them, 'proper' bathrooms were an important part of the ideal Federation house.

Robert Haddon suggested that:

SMALL SUBURBAN VILLA

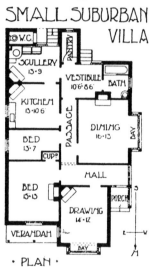

· PLAN ·

Servants had already disappeared; while rising construction costs meant that by 1908 the suburban 'villa' was little more than a decorated box.
HADDON, *AUSTRALIAN ARCHITECTURE*

The walls and floor should be of tiles, white predominating, with a touch of cool sea green or china blue, and with all corners rounded. The bath should not be encased, but open all round for light, air, and cleansing, and of cast iron fired, white enamelled, and with nickel fittings . . . For towel rails . . . nickel is best . . . For floor mats, open rubber, cork, or wood open gratings may be used. Soap and sponge cages should all be of open work, nickelled, and hung to the sides of the bath. The lavatory basin should . . . be quite open, all parts free from casing, and all of the visible metal may be nickelled.[14]

One of Haddon's published designs for a typical small suburban villa shows the bathroom, kitchen, laundry and WC all included under one roof, thereby doing away with the skillions and outbuildings of earlier times.

As domestic help gradually became scarce and expensive, much attention was focussed on the kitchen. As early as 1902 architect John Sulman ventured to predict that 'middle class households will, in the future, have to dispense with servants altogether'. By 1914, *Home and Garden Beautiful* magazine was discussing design details for 'the servantless house', placing an emphasis on compactness and convenience:

Glance at the working part of every house (the kitchen) and you will find, in nine cases out of ten, a dismal place, badly lit and ventilated, badly arranged, very hard to keep clean, and a long tramp to the dining room. A kitchen needs plenty of light, and plenty of ventilation. The pantry must be close handy, and also well lit and ventilated. White tiles should be placed around the stove, and, if possible, on the walls, and in the case of wooden

Change was slow to affect life on Outback stations, and servants (from left: cook, housemaid and parlourmaid) could still be employed for £60 per year.
MITCHELL LIBRARY

153

houses, a dado of stamped steel, enamelled white. All woodwork, shelves, etc., should be white enamelled, and the floor, if possible, covered with such a material as permasite. Add to these conveniences, such as power for electric iron, gas or electric stove, etc., and you have a kitchen that is a pleasure, in place of a constant eyesore.

The absence of servants meant there were other things for well bred women to talk about besides croquet and the weather. Eva Daniel, writing about her family in the 1900s, mentions in passing that: 'Women in those days always discussed their sweeping problems; some advocated sprinkling damp tea leaves to catch the dust. Elizabeth was among the first in Maldon to acquire a Bissell's carpet sweeper.'[15]

Labour-saving devices, designed to replace servants and make life easier for the 'housewife', included electric jugs, irons, toasters and stoves, gas heaters for water in the bathroom and kitchen, and gas fires or electric radiators for interior heating. Most houses were lit by gas or electricity while, in the country, kerosene or tungsten carbide lamps still glowed in the darkness: 'at night sometimes we'd have a game of euchre; mostly though we put our spare time into fancy-work of different kinds, all done by kerosene lamps. We did have an Edison phonograph and a shelf of cylinders from the top to the bottom of the wall.'[16]

The Edison phonograph had introduced even the most remote home to the dubious benefits of American culture. It was a radical change from the influence of Britain; America was brassy, modern, progressive, the source of the new vacuum cleaner and all the latest ideas. American books and popular magazines began to appear, and from this unlikely source came the architectural influences that would alter once more the face of Australian suburbia:

We bought American magazines and many of them had house plans and photos published every month, particularly the Ladies' Home Journal; thus was introduced the Californian bungalow, or 'bungle-oh', as some called it. It had some good

points; it freed the small house from the drawing room, introducing the idea of a living room connected to the kitchen by a door, introduced the breakfast ingle and built in furniture. The domestic servant had quite disappeared for most people and the house plan was adjusted. The kitchen had good cupboards, the pantry disappeared, so did the scullery; instead there was a small wash house or laundry often as a separate outbuilding. The kitchen became a room the housewife could ask her friends to enter. The chief defect of the bungalow to my mind was a certain heavy clumsy look inherited from the crude furniture and buildings of the Spanish Mission days in California; a verandah post had to be of brick and large enough to carry a two storey house, wooden beams were unnecessarily large, an open fireplace ran up to the ceiling in heavy tuckpointed brick and occupied quite a large slice of many a small room.[17]

The bungalow was not merely a style; it was the beginning of the creative marketing of housing. Articles on the bungalow began to evoke emotive images of a whole new stress-free lifestyle which would magically suffuse its occupants with a feeling of well-being. This was something that other houses simply did not have: 'A Cottage is a little house in the country but a Bungalow is a little country house, a homely little place, with verandahs and balconies, and the plan so arranged as to ensure complete comfort with a feeling of rusticity and ease.'[18]

Even the trade journal *Building* spoke in glowing terms of simple furniture, rugs and cushions scattered on the floor, wide fireplaces built of rubble and chimneys of rough, moss-stained stones, 'with a log fire blazing on the big hearth, and oneself stretched on a rug before it, well provided with good books and tobacco, it matters not how the wind blows nor what the world thinks'.[19] In 1915 the prospect appealed to many, among them young George Foletta:

I had always been creative, and many of my friends were among the artists of the day. There were some of my acquaintances in church circles who

Refrigeration was in wide commercial use by 1908, but was yet to penetrate the domestic market. The most effective method of keeping food fresh was still the zinc-lined wooden ice chest.

Facing page
'Women in those days,' wrote Eva Daniel of life in the early 1900s, 'always discussed their sweeping problems' — obviously a matter of great interest in an era of floor-length white skirts.
BATTYE LIBRARY

So new its front lawn is still a gardener's dream, this neat Californian bungalow was the epitome of style around 1914. The overhanging eaves and deep verandahs were sensible design elements.
BATTYE LIBRARY

may have thought me Bohemian. However, I was just an ordinary, forward-looking young fellow who happened to be a good draughtsman. I was determined to break with convention and build a home of my own design.

In those days, depending on the working man's income, he either rented a home in built up suburbs like Carlton and South Melbourne, or purchased on terms one of the new double fronted weatherboard homes which 'spec' builders were erecting on the periphery of what are now inner suburbs.

There are hundreds of these small homes still standing today in all the nearby suburbs; most of them built on relatively small blocks with 35' or 50' frontages, and few with more than 20' of garden

between the house and the street. People with prospects and a little more money built more elaborate, but not dissimilar, homes on larger blocks of land in the then expanding middle-class suburbs such as Malvern, Essendon, etc.

Whether they were the small weatherboard homes costing between three and four hundred pounds, or the larger brick houses in the better suburbs, they were mostly variations of the same type of architecture — double fronted, with bay windows, narrow verandahs, and rooms on either side of a passage.

The American magazines then coming to Australia were featuring the new Californian bungalows. These attractive houses appealed to us with

156

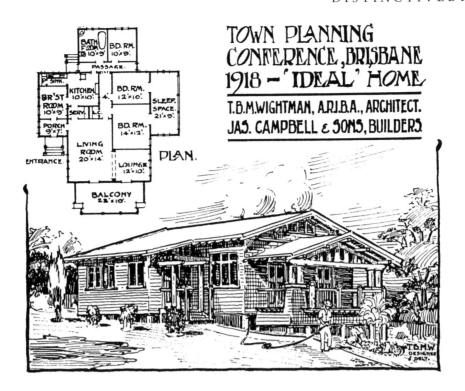

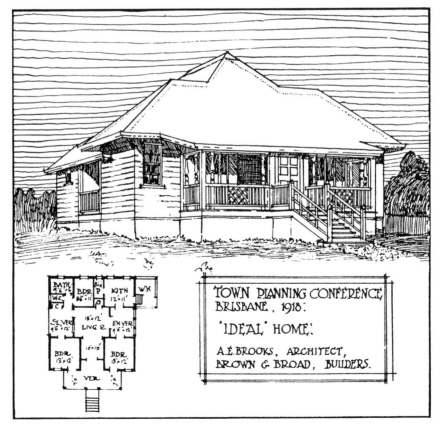

The promise of a more rational world after 1918 was reflected in house designs tailored to both climate and finance.

As always, patriotism was strongest among those in the position to profit least from war. A Leichhardt, Sydney, mother and father pose with their Digger son in 1918, outside their home.
HISTORIC PHOTOGRAPH RESOURCE CENTRE

their wide eaves and spacious verandahs, on to which opened at least one large living room. They were far better suited to Australia's sunny climate, and for entertaining, than the homes of our parents, based on the English idea of a long passage and a stuffy little drawing room.

The bungalow we had designed was to have a 22' panelled living room with a dining annexe and a sizeable main bedroom, both with double doors opening to a wide verandah.[20]

A bungalow design was considered the 'Ideal Home' at the second Australian town planning conference, held in Brisbane in July 1918, and the State Savings Bank of South Australia soon produced a series of simple bungalow plans suitable for the soldiers returning from the Great War.

Private enterprise, patriotic as ever, was also anxious to help. 'Returned Men! Why not own a bit of the country you fought for?' ran the advertising for Sydney's new Burwood Park Estate. It was a fine proposition for those who could afford it. Those who could not waited patiently for the 'homes fit for heroes' which they had been promised. For some it would be a long wait.

Returned servicemen often had to move to find work, and the solution for some was simply to take their houses with them, towed by a puffing — and agonisingly slow — steam traction engine.
MUSEUM OF VICTORIA

TIMBER   HOME

Erected at Yeronga.   Cost £740.

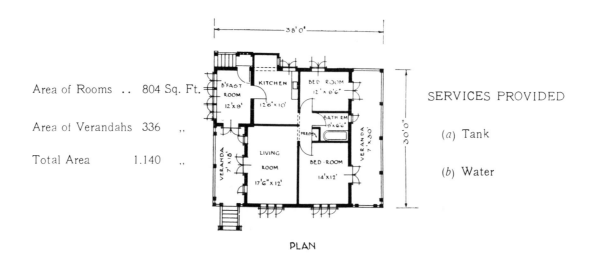

Area of Rooms .. 804 Sq. Ft.

Area of Verandahs 336   ,,

Total Area   1,140   ,,

SERVICES PROVIDED

(a) Tank

(b) Water

PLAN

'Our Bungalow of Dreams' 1920-1940

When I got started building the house and I got to the floor joists I said to Mum,
'God, this house'll never get built'; because I'd never built a house
in my life before, you know.

Stanley Diss, soldier settler in Western Australia, 1920

ALL OVER AUSTRALIA VARIOUS SCHEMES HAD BEGUN to settle ex-soldiers and their families on farms and orchards of their own, but in most cases the lots were too small to be viable and the amount of capital available to develop them, insufficient. Coupled with the inexperience of the average soldier settler, this meant that, for many, their years of work brought nothing but disillusionment and eventual bankruptcy. By 1927, one third of the soldier settlers had walked off the land.

Stanley Diss, who took up a block at Burracoppin, Western Australia, in 1920, said that the £150 'repat' money allotted for his house was not enough even to pay for the building materials. As a result, for some time the house had timber floor in two rooms while the other two had none. This lead to some inconvenience. Diss reported that one day he returned from hunting rabbits to discover:

The chooks had come under the floor, where there was no floor, and had got into the room where there was floor, up on the kitchen table, and they'd scratched, eaten the bread, the butter, everything . . . oh, all over the place. That was the end of that; we had to build a chook house then, to keep 'em in.[1]

Elsewhere, other novice farmers were having similar learning experiences. The group settlement scheme devised by the West Australian government established groups of twenty or thirty families to develop and fence all their blocks together before acquiring individual titles and houses.

It was a life with few creature comforts, leaving plenty of scope for improvisation. One of the most commonly available raw materials was the kerosene box. Elsie Firth recalls:

For lighting purposes we used kerosene. It was purchased in four-gallon tins, two tins to a case. Both tins and cases were of good quality and proved very useful. Many a settler's cottage was partly furnished with furniture made from these cases, and our home was no exception.

Seven cases stacked on top of each other and placed a certain distance from the wall, with a rod extending from the cases to the wall to provide hanging space; a coat of paint to the side, and a curtain hung in front of the whole and you had a very serviceable and quite neat wardrobe. With a little ingenuity many pieces of furniture could be made thus. As for the kero tins, their uses were endless.[2]

So useful that in 1925 the New Settlers League of Australia published a booklet called *Makeshifts*, containing 1000 designs for furniture and kitchen utensils made from kerosene tins and cases. The sponsoring oil companies were delighted — it was kerosene culture par excellence.

In more esoteric circles, the cube had fallen into disrepute as a design element. The avant-garde Futurist movement released a manifesto, in the

Facing page
The War Service Homes scheme assisted many returned servicemen to purchase their own homes. But home ownership on a budget meant some conveniences had to wait; in the case of this 1923 War Service home at Yeronga, Qld, the toilet and laundry were both beneath the house.
JOHN OXLEY LIBRARY

161

Above: West Australian war veterans were offered land and pre-cut houses by the government. On occasion a family of ten had to fit into a house that wasn't designed for expansion or modification.
BATTYE LIBRARY

Right: tea in the kitchen on a Sunday afternoon was a rare pleasure for the group settler who spent six hard days a week trying to scrape a living — and a future for his family — from a block of land which was usually too small and often in marginal country.

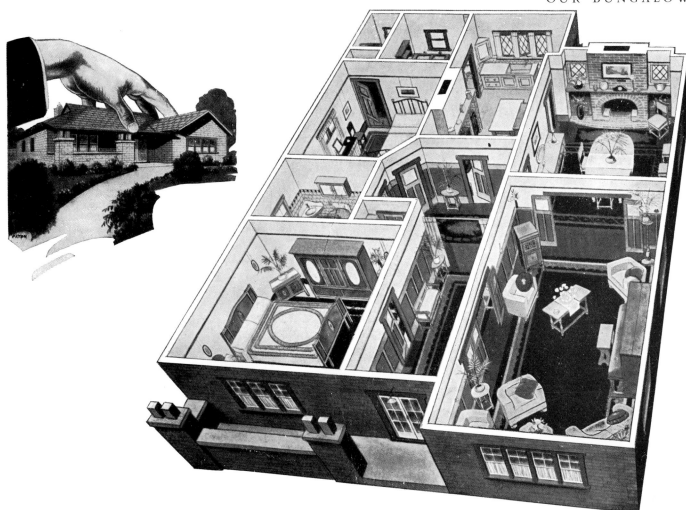

magazine in 1921, which spoke of spherical houses drifting about like helium-filled balloons. They called this 'Mechanical Nomadism':

The houses, free and detachable from their fixed foundations shall soar high into the heavens, to descend again in due course gracefully to earth, drawn by the force of gravity.

Each house will be so constructed that its several rooms shall be detachable, like railway carriages. A room, when so detached, will be picked up by a powerful aerial machine and transported from one place to another — from Rome, let us say, to New York — in one night's journey.

Of course the entrance to the house will be through the roof, where hangars for every kind of air-craft will be provided. No elevators, no stair-case will be necessary even though the house may have a hundred stories. The kitchen will always be at the bottom of the house, whence the meals will be brought up automatically to the table.

The cubic form of the old-fashioned house has persisted hitherto because it economises space and material. In the coming age we shall build houses conical or spherical — never cubical. We shall despise the repetition of windows or columns, and shall electrocute any artist or architect who employs the same idea more than once.[3]

Had the Futurists the power to put their ideas into practice, the continuing popularity of the Californian bungalow — now known simply as the Bungalow style — would have led to an orgy of electrocution in suburbia.

The bungalow had enjoyed a brief period of fashionable acceptance amongst those in the forefront of progress, before it was adapted for mass production by builders everywhere. The approved

An unusual insight into the layout and decor of the 1920s bungalow. Plywood panelling is used extensively in the entrance hall and in the sitting room which opens into a cosy dining room.
AUSTRALIAN HOME BEAUTIFUL MAY 1923

formula had rough-cast exterior walls, the wide low-pitched roof was tiled, the double gable ends were shingled, and heavy tapered pillars supported the low porch roof. Inside, stained plywood panelling, exposed timber beams, polished wooden floors, and small casement windows created a dark restful atmosphere where it was supposed romance, like mushrooms, might flourish in the shadows.

A popular song of the day, 'Bungalow of Dreams', by the great Bix Beiderbecke, summed up its charms:

Our little love nest
Beside a stream
Where red, red roses grow
Our bungalow
Of dreams

Far from the city
Somehow it seems
We're sitting pretty in
Our bungalow
Of dreams

Just like two love birds
We'll bill and coo
I'll whisper love words
For only you

A bit of heaven
Beside a stream
I know you'll love it so
Our bungalow
Of dreams

The magazine *Real Property Annual* (which would become the influential *Australian Home Beautiful*) commented on the bungalow mania in 1921:

In the newer suburbs ... streets upon streets of these houses have been built ... The similarity of these cottages ... is indeed remarkable ... To the discriminating eye this resemblance in design is rather monotonous, but it is nevertheless a welcome contrast to the hideous two-storey houses of the late seventies and early eighties which mar so many of the older suburbs.[4]

Even in the wilds of the tropical north, fashion prevailed:

Some of the most remarkable aboriginal homes to be seen anywhere in Australia are at Cowal Creek, near the inner tip of the Cape York Peninsula, where the natives have erected very comfortable bark homes built on the bungalow plan of the white man in the north. The houses are on high stumps and have wide verandas, but not a stick of sawn timber has been used in any of the dwellings;

Above: the International school's break with tradition seems all the more radical when houses such as this are examined: elements of the Federation style, such as small-paned windows and roof finials, could still be seen in the Californian bungalow.
BATTYE LIBRARY

Left: the brick piers of this 1930s house overlooking Sydney Harbour may have improved the occupants' view, but their lack of design destroyed any potential for successful interpretation of the bungalow ideal.
MUSEUM OF VICTORIA

they have a framework of saplings, with walls, roof, and floor of slabs of bark.[5]

The rectangular shape of the bungalow worked most effectively with its front facing the road, and this lead to a demand for wider building blocks. Where previously the average suburban block had a 13-metre frontage, it was now gradually increased to 16 metres.

Then the new motor car needed a home of its own. It was assumed that the garage, like the displaced horse's stable, should be set a respectable distance from the house. This usually necessitated a driveway at the side of the house, adding another 3 metres or so to the width of the block. The 19-metre-wide block soon became the standard for subdivisions.

The next fashion to follow the bungalow was the Spanish Mission, another import from California — though this time an Englishman was the catalyst. Leslie Wilkinson arrived at Sydney University in 1921 to become Australia's first professor of architecture. In the following year he built a Spanish style home for himself at Vaucluse and advocated its general suitability. Several interesting examples were built before this style, too, was reduced to a 'spec' builder's formula.

True Spanish Mission houses, with their thick white-painted walls and shady enclosed courtyards and loggias, would have been ideal in many parts of Australia. Unfortunately, the 'Mission' of the suburbs was often no more than a new style of icing on the same old cake: rounded arches with candy-twist pillars, arched windows with wrought iron grilles, a tiled porch, semi-circular Cordova tiles on the roof and chimney, and external walls coated with cream stucco.

One attractive example of suburban Spanish style was built at Southport, Queensland, by Robert Johnston, as a home for his new bride, Lila. It

was revolutionary in 1936, according to Lila, and the locals did not know what to make of it:

One day I went to the letter box and a woman passing by said, 'What are you doing here?' I was very annoyed. I said, 'I live here', and she replied that she thought my house was a church. Someone else thought it was a morgue.[6]

To avoid further confusion Robert named the house Santa Nita, after one of the ships of the Armada defeated by Drake. The name was written on two swords worked into the stucco front wall.

House names were a popular talking point during the 1920s. M.K. Smyth, in an article 'On Naming Your Home', begged her readers to show their patriotism on their front gates by using Australian names instead of English ones:

The Australian language provides us with a whole dictionary of soft, attractive, musical and mystifying names.

Call your home 'Wirringulla' (Home of Happiness) and conceal the fact from the passer-by that you occasionally pitch a dinner-plate at your wife's head. Or call it 'Carawatta' or 'Currawarra' and save people the trouble of looking for the pine tree that you don't possess.

'Cooloongatta' is a better camouflage than 'Bellevue' if you want to crack hardy and pretend you admire the hoardings, and 'Lanacoona' (Home of the Kangaroo) will guard the secret that you lack a marsupial from all save the initiated.[7]

Arriving in Australia in 1922, the writer D.H. Lawrence was fascinated by this preoccupation. Somers, the hero of his novel *Kangaroo*, arrives fresh off the boat so to speak, at 'Murdoch Street', Sydney:

an old sort of suburb, little squat bungalows with corrugated iron roofs, painted red. Each little bungalow was set in its own hand-breadth of

Robert Johnston's Santa Nita, built at Southport, Qld, in 1936, had such a revolutionary facade that unsuspecting passersby at first mistook it for a church or funeral parlour.
JOHN ARCHER

167

ground, surrounded by a little wooden palisade fence. And there went the long street, like a child's drawing, the little square bungalows dot-dot-dot, close together and yet apart, like modern democracy, each one fenced round with a square rail fence. The street was wide, and strips of worn grass took the place of kerb-stones. The stretch of macadam in the middle seemed as forsaken as a desert, as the hansom clock-clocked along it.

Fifty-one had its name painted by the door. Somers had been watching these names. He had passed 'Elite', and 'Très Bon' and 'The Angels of Roost' and 'The Better 'Ole'. He rather hoped for one of the Australian names. Wallamby or Wagga-Wagga. When he had looked at the house and agreed to take it for three months, it had been dusk, and he had not noticed the name. He hoped it would not be U-An-Me, or even Stella Maris.

'Forestin,' he said, reading the flourishing T as an F. 'What language do you imagine that is?'

'It's T, not F,' said Harriet.

'Torestin,' he said, pronouncing it like Russian. 'Must be a native word.'

'No,' said Hariet. 'it means To rest in,' She didn't even laugh at him. [8]

An acute observer of his environment, Lawrence included in Kangaroo this detailed description of an outer Sydney suburb at dusk:

But, oh, the deep mystery of joy it was to him to sit at the edge of the bush as twilight fell, and look down at the township. The bungalows were built mostly on the sides of the slopes. They had no foundations, but stood on brickwork props, which brought them up to the level. There they stood on the hillsides, on their short legs, with darkness under their floors, the little bungalows, looking as if they weighed nothing. Looking flimsy, made of wood with corrugated zinc roofs. Some of them were painted dark red, roofs and all, some were painted grey, some were wooden simply. Many had the white-grey zinc roofs, pale and delicate. At the back was always one big water-butt of corrugated iron, a big round tank painted dark-red, the corrugation ribs running round, and a jerky, red-painted pipe coming down from the eaves. Sometimes there were two of these tanks: and a thin, not very tidy woman in a big straw hat stooping to the tap at the bottom of the tank. The roof came down low, making a long shade over the wooden verandas. Nearly always a little loggia at the back, from which the house door opened. And this little verandah was the woman's kitchen; there she had a little table with her dirty dishes, which she was going to wash up. And a cat would be trotting around, as if it had not an enemy in the world, while from the verandah a parrot called. [9]

Many homes had a wireless, a large walnut veneer box with a panel of tan silk mesh down the front from which issued the voice of Richard Tauber or popular songs — perhaps even 'Barney Google with the Goo Goo Googley Eyes'. The piano still served as an instrument for home entertainment, although some homes had the latest pianola:

Our cousins, who lived far out in the bush, worked and scrimped and saved to buy a pianola . . . Going for holidays to Auntie Ivy's became a new pleasure for which we completed eagerly. To sit at that pianola and produce bright intricate musical performances, just by pedalling vigorously, was an experience to boast about for weeks to come . . .

It cost several hundred pounds, and perhaps it would indicate the deep desire for some sort of lightness in a drab life when we remember that this highly-polished new-fangled invention was carted by horse-wagon to a house which had never known running water, a conventional bath-tub or a kitchen sink. [10]

The more modern houses now had quite well-equipped kitchens. Kitchen furniture — dressers, tables and so on — was gradually being replaced by built-in benches and cupboards; the ice chest and the safe were also about to be superseded. Sir Edward Hallstrom produced his first small home refrigerator in 1924, and by 1936 his kerosene powered models, independent of electric power, had spread throughout the country.

Kelvinator, meanwhile, was advertising that its rather cumbersome and expensive 1925-model

There's New Enjoyment in Foods from the—
Zone of Kelvination

It requires a temperature *below 50 deg.* –all the time– to keep foods properly. Kelvination maintains this.

Thick steaks that almost melt in your mouth; green salads so crisp they fall apart at the touch of a fork!

You have often wondered how these and other foods are so deliciously prepared and attractively served in the best hotels. There is no real secret about it. The foods you, yourself, buy will acquire the same delicious qualities under the influence of the Zone of Kelvination.

Kelvinator—the electric method for chilling refrigerators without ice—creates a condition in any refrigerator that affects foods in a remarkable way. It reduces the temperature to 10 degrees colder than when it is ice cooled, but does something more. It crystallizes the moisture out of the refrigerator, leaving the interior not only cold but *dry.* All moisture disappears. The air takes on a sharp, frosty "sting."

Under the influence of this Kelvinated air, foods not only stay fresh and sweet for *days,* but actually *improve.* Meats mellow and acquire a delicious tenderness. Green vegetables "crisp up" and are better than when fresh from the garden New frozen dainties can be prepared that will delight your family and amaze your guests.

You can install Kelvinator in your present refrigerator and be prepared for every occasion; family dinner or entertainment. You will escape forever the annoyances of ice delivery, as Kelvinator refrigerates for months or years without attention. You can keep a liberal supply of food on hand, and market only once a week. And with all these advantages, Kelvinator is an actual economy.

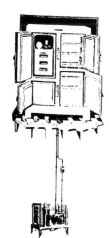

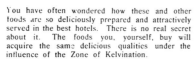

Kelvinator
The Oldest Domestic Electric Refrigeration

N.S.W.: DUE & LEQUESNE PTY. LTD., 15 Bligh St., SYDNEY.
VICTORIA: DUE & LEQUESNE PTY. LTD., 527 Collins St., MELBOURNE.
W. A. CROWLE LTD. *Factory Representatives.-* Crowle House, Castlereagh St., SYDNEY, N.S.W.
Agents wanted where not represented.

More efficient than the ice chest, the refrigerator became a common feature of the Australian home in the 1920s; a week's worth of food could be stored in its 'Zone of Kelvination'.
MELBOURNE PUNCH 1925

The claims made by advertisements have never reflected too close a relationship with reality: the 'freedom from domestic drudgery' to be achieved when cooking on a wood-burning stove is questionable, while kerosene's miraculous properties cannot mask its odour.

electric refrigerator even possessed miraculous properties. In the Zone of Kelvination: 'foods not only stay fresh and sweet for days but actually improve. Meats mellow and acquire a delicious tenderness. Green vegetables "crisp up" and are better than when fresh from the garden.'

In the early 1920s the *Home* was the modern Australian magazine for the new breed of housewife. In an article in June 1920, titled 'The Core of the Home — the Kitchen', Mrs Fred Aronsen summarised the changes that were taking place:

The great prominence given to kitchens, utensils, cookery and kindred subjects in recent years is doubtless due to the changed conditions with regard to domestic service brought about by the absorption into factories and other business places, of the class from which such service was drawn.

Scarcity of servants means their replacement in the average suburban home by the one-time mistress. It means also that the average young bride must spend a great part of her time in the kitchen. Thus has a revolution in Kitchendom been brought about, because one finds out by personal exper-

ience things that had not occurred to one before. One knows now, without a doubt, that when working and cooking in a kitchen one must have air, light, space, and more than usual convenience. To meet this demand the papers are full of advertisements of up-to-date labour-saving devices.[11]

Although lacking in subtlety, these early advertisements were the beginning of a new type of sales pitch: 'To husbands who want their wives to stay young, when you say "This is my wife", you want to introduce a woman who looks fresh, youthful and happy — not old or worn or tired. Well, here's your chance to help her look young!' The answer — the new Easy electric washer: 'Sixteen double sheets handled at one time — think of that!'

In a similar vein was General Electric's vision of female liberation:

Yesterday! The kitchen clock tolls away a woman's life. Toil worn hands, scarred by labor, monotonously dip-dip into a greasy dish pan. A roaring fire, kept burning to heat the water and cook the next meal, smothers the room under a blanket of hot

Above: the 'Model Kitchen' of 1920 offered the two-door Special Safe, the Quick Meal Gas Stove, the 'Gem' dresser ('embracing almost every conceivable labour saving device known to the culinary art'), the Kosciusko ice chest, and a linoleum floor. *HOME* SEPT 1920

Burley Griffin's designs taught Australians to see their country — and their homes — in new ways. Although he did not attempt to disguise the 'machinery' of his houses, he related them to their settings by, for example, doing away with the dominant mass of a conventional sloping roof. This is the house Griffin built for himself at Castlecrag.
MAX DUPAIN

motionless air. Dim, fitful light shadows and multiplies the laboured motions of a drooping figure. Each day is but a repetition of the day before ... a monotonous routine commanding woman's time, demanding her presence and shutting out all but a brief hour or two that she can call her own. There is little need of a clock in this old-fashioned kitchen for time is not measured here by minutes or hours, but by drab days ... days that leave the inescapable marks of kitchen toil.

Today! A youthful hand that defies the years, touches a switch and a brilliant room is flooded with light. Clean, beautiful, efficient ... every inch of this kitchen is arranged to save woman's steps. Magic electric servants work for her ... she DIRECTS and they DO. Her days are her own ... her hours are free! World progress is marked and measured by man's success in lifting the burdens of daily life from his family, and there has been no greater achievement than that of vanquishing the

dreary hours of household drudgery. Truly, freedom has come to our womenfolk. [12]

In years to come the precise nature of this 'freedom' would often be called into question.

One woman who never expressed any doubts about the nature of equality was house and landscape designer Edna Walling. In the 1920s she began to develop her own village at Mooroolbark on the outskirts of Melbourne. Here, Walling saw an opportunity to create an ideal subdivision based on environmental and aesthetic principles. She sold land only to those who would accept a house and garden design she prepared for them.

At that stage her inspiration came from the rural English landscape, with its stone cottages and informal gardens. Walling was herself a passionate builder who knew exactly what she wanted. When someone questioned the low stone walls of her studio, she replied impatiently: 'We did not build them higher than six feet because we like them six feet high!'

Dismissing the prevailing architectural fashions as pragmatic and uninspiring, Walling advised:

Not that good design costs any more, but rather that the truth is we have become accustomed to the mediocre and thus the repetition goes on and will go on until we spend as much thought and consideration on the exterior as we do to ensure that the plan is functional. The pitch of the roof, the height of the walls, the design, dimensions and decorations of doorways, and colour, are all things of equal importance.

We must not overlook either, the great consequence of design in the windows and see that they are good in proportion, not merely the opening but the size and proportion of the lights (the individual panes of glass). Their disposition so that every good outlook is taken advantage of should help greatly in giving individuality to the cottage design.[13]

Another subdivision where the emphasis was on individuality was the model Sydney suburb of Castlecrag. This was conceived by the American architect and planner, Walter Burley Griffin; like Walling he either designed or approved the houses so they were in accordance with his vision: 'in harmony with the great amphitheatre of stone and forest.'

Griffin had originally come to Australia to be director of design for the Federal capital being built at Canberra, but the position was so poorly paid that in order to survive financially other projects were necessary. In 1927, with a group of Melbourne investors, Griffin bought steeply sloping property overlooking Sydney's Middle Harbour and excercised careful control over the development. A protégé of the great American architect Frank Lloyd Wright, Griffin was an original thinker who produced his own style of small intimate houses:

Low, square masses of stone or concrete block, they merge naturally into the terraced bluffs.

Above: owing more to the philosophies of Frank Lloyd Wright than to local architecture, Walter Burley Griffin's houses introduced light and undisguised natural materials to the suburban home.
AUSTRALIAN HANDBOOK APRIL 1928

Left: a Canberra house under construction in the 1930s. Although building with concrete blocks was labour intensive, even a large residence could be finished quickly and efficiently.
AUSTRALIAN ARCHIVES

Their windows are all sizes, from narrow casements to wide unbroken sheets of glass giving stunning views of the harbour. Inside walls were finished in rough plaster, coloured in sunny tints or yellows and buffs. Chimneys are huge affairs of solid stone, and the kitchens had double-sinks, then a novelty in Australia.[14]

Unfortunately, the plans for Castlecrag were set back somewhat by the Great Depression. Other developers suffered a similar fate. John Gawler recalls that:

In a very short time the building trade became stagnant; houses and other buildings in course of erection were stopped. A melancholy sight often seen on a Sunday afternoon stroll was the timber frame of a house darkened by age with tall weeds growing up through the bare bones of the floor. We all suffered, thousands of building tradesmen were out of work, builders went bankrupt, architects found other work if possible, timber yards were jammed with scantlings whilst machinery rusted, brickyards had eight million bricks 'at grass', a queer way of stating that bricks were stacked in open yards where there was certainly little grass; I believe it is an old English expression dating back for centuries. Many houses in the outer suburbs had 'For Sale' or 'To Let' notices up, gardens grew ragged and houses soon began to look down at heel.[15]

But there was always a place for an entrepreneur with a sense of timing. Such a one was Mr Daley of Whittlesea, 50 kilometres from Melbourne, who like Walling and Griffin created his own suburb, at 'Blackwood Park'. An early exercise in functional Depression architecture, Blackwood Park consisted of seventeen disused railway carriages, each on its own plot of land and let to selected tenants for £1 per week. They were not a bad bargain for the price, if this visitor's description was accurate:

The 'carriage' is now a most comfortable residence. A little porch opens into a beautifully furnished living room with a comfortable suite, dining table, a wireless cabinet, several good pictures, a carpet and floor-rugs, and a most impressive pair of antlers over the door leading to the bedroom. This was another dainty apartment with a fine double bed and a wardrobe plus the usual bedroom paraphernalia. There were four rooms, in all, each leading out of the other. Besides the double-bed room, there was one with a single bed, a kitchen, and the living-room already referred to — which, by the way is 18 feet by 9. Nowhere was there a sense of being 'cabin'd, cribb'd and confin'd'.

There was a well-appointed porcelain bath, with water laid on, a sink in the kitchen, also with running water, a built-in pantry, a pot-cupboard, a drip-board. There was even a linen press in the snug little home.

And above this ideal nest the birds were chattering and chattering and the kookaburras laughing for the very joy of things.[16]

For humans, however, it was not a particularly joyful period. Because they were unable to keep up their payments, many unemployed families lost homes they had recently bought, and tenants were evicted from houses when they could not pay their rent.

The 1933 census showed that 33 000 people were on the road in the middle of winter, while a further 400 000 were living in homes made of iron, calico, canvas, bark, hessian and other scavenged materials. Often these were clustered together in camps such as Happy Valley, in the sand dunes of Botany Bay. With admirable sensitivity Lady Game, the wife of the governor of New South Wales, said after a visit to Happy Valley that she saw one little home she would not mind living in herself. Its

With admirable restraint, the Melbourne and Metropolitan Tramways Board advertised trams for sale as 'sleep-outs, garden shelters, bathing boxes, forcing houses, etc.'
— not as houses.
AUSTRALIAN HOME BEAUTIFUL 1 MAR 1930

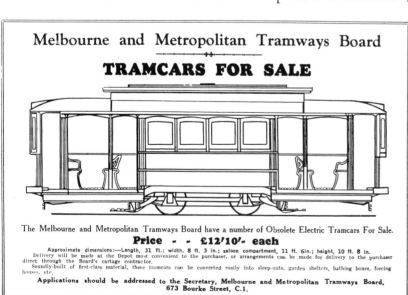

Melbourne and Metropolitan Tramways Board

TRAMCARS FOR SALE

The Melbourne and Metropolitan Tramways Board have a number of Obsolete Electric Tramcars For Sale.

Price - - £12'10'- each

Approximate dimensions:—Length, 31 ft.; width, 8 ft. 3 in.; saloon compartment, 11 ft. 6in.; height, 10 ft. 8 in.

Delivery will be made at the Depot most convenient to the purchaser, or arrangements can be made for delivery to the purchaser direct through the Board's cartage contractor.

Soundly-built of first-class material, these tramcars can be converted easily into sleep-outs, garden shelters, bathing boxes, forcing houses, etc.

Applications should be addressed to the Secretary, Melbourne and Metropolitan Tramways Board, 673 Bourke Street, C.1.

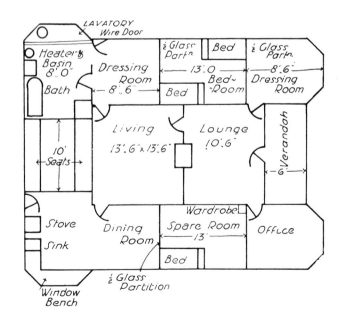

Above: unemployment also meant materials were scarce and expensive, so ingenuity came to the fore in such gypsy-caravan dwellings as this recycled tram 'Bungalow' at Yanchep, WA.
BATTYE LIBRARY

Left: retired tramway engineer Noel Richards bought three secondhand trams (total cost £37 10s) and made a 'picturesque, comfortable and conven-ient' home for himself and his wife.
AUSTRALIAN HOME BEAUTIFUL 1 MAR 1930

175

Above: forced out of their own home, an unemployed family in Gippsland, Vic, shelters in a bark humpy while the breadwinner searchers the 'Positions Vacant' column in vain.
BAIRNSDALE HISTORICAL SOCIETY

Right: homeless people squatted on land adjacent to the rubbish tip in Dudley Street, West Melbourne, during the Depression; their huts, the Dudley Mansions, were built from salvaged materials.
LATROBE LIBRARY

A feature of street life in the 1930s was home delivery — in this case, straight to the kitchen — of bread, milk and eggs. Many office workers or tradespeople were glad of such employment.

Above: protected by his dog, his determination — and a case of Nobel's gelignite — Swedish immigrant Edward Dolph weathered the Depression in a hollow log in the Gippsland forest.

Facing page
A.V. (Bert) Jennings brought together builders and designers to produce comfortable houses that were still within reach of Depression homebuyers. This, his first, cost £895 in 1932.
A.V. JENNINGS PTY LTD

owners pointed out to a reporter that they would be only too happy to swap.

Obviously many people managed to retain their sense of humour. Bert Jennings, in search of potential partners for his infant building business, recalls:

One builder, when I visited him to offer him a job, was running a few fowls for food and immediately began counting his fowls. When I asked him the reason, he said that usually after he had a visitor there was a fowl missing.[17]

Observing that there were some discerning cash buyers still in the market, Jennings set out to design a home that would attract them. Eventually he found that for £895 he could produce a fully equipped brick house on its own land. He sold nine of these homes during 1932, his first year of operation, and by 1938 Jennings was developing large estates with remarkable success.

The houses Jennings was marketing with such skill were conservative in design, but by 1934 there was a new influence at work among younger architects which would gradually spread to the suburbs. The new watchword was Functionalism.

The French philosopher-architect Charles Jeanneret ('Le Corbusier') had described the house as a 'machine for living'. This became an important theme of the Modern or International style, accompanied by an obsession with efficiency. Design for function became a high priority. The kitchen, for example, was now stripped of all romance:

The kitchen is really a factory in miniature, for in it materials are manufactured into the various dishes that go to make up the meals enjoyed by the members of the household. In factory planning it is essential to arrange the various departments so that the article in course of production passes in an orderly manner from process to process, right from the entry of the raw materials to the delivery of the finished article at the loading platform; in dealing with the kitchen the same kind of care must be taken.[18]

Above: the return of good times, work, and readily available materials as the economic depression eased saw an explosion of grandiose building, such as this mock Tudor 'mansionette' in Perth. BATTYE LIBRARY

Right: Tudor interiors were dark and as ponderous as the house facades, with stained half-timbered beams over joins in the fibrous plaster wall-panelling and mass-produced 'craftsman' furnishings. BATTYE LIBRARY

Above: in the same house, the living room featured an incongruous mixture of chromed steel and Tudor style sideboards. Glass doors overcame some of the gloom produced by small windows.
BATTYE LIBRARY

Left: a symphony in curvilinear veneer, the master bedroom at least gave its fashion-conscious occupants some relief from the period look of the remainder of the house.
BATTYE LIBRARY

Student architect Mary Turner Shaw painted an amusing picture of the Functionalist house in her 1935 revue song, 'When We Build a Modern Home':

There's a bright vermilion door,
With a chromium plated handle;
We create a little scandal
When we build a modern home.

There's a cantilever sun porch,
With a green and yellow awning;
Where we sun-bathe in the morning,
When we build a modern home.

There's some concrete and some steel-work,
But most of all the walls are glass;
But the painter does the real work,
And the rest keep off the grass.

We'll have rubber on the floor,
And a sound-absorbent ceiling;
There's contemporary feeling
In our very modern home.

Diametrically opposed to this Functionalist approach were the Romantics, including José Paronella, a Spanish immigrant who made his fortune in sugarcane and afterwards returned to Spain to find a bride with whom he could share his retirement on an estate of his dreams. Although he found a bride he missed his adopted home, so in 1929 he arrived back at Innisfail in north Queensland, bought 9 hectares of jungle and began to build a mansion. Paronella Park took more than twenty years to construct and, although José had no experience in landscaping or architecture, he managed to build one of the most unusual homes in the north.

Outside Melbourne, in the mid 1930s, another Romantic, artist and architect Justus Jorgensen, with the help of some friends, began to create his own vision of a mediaeval manor farm from earth and stone; the nearby country village of Eltham would never be the same again.

Unfortunately, the debate between the Romantics and the Functionalists was interrupted by the outbreak of war. It seemed appropriate to postpone further discussion.

Above: Spanish immigrant José Paronella designed and built an eclectic concrete fantasy near Innisfail, Qld. Power was supplied by Paronella's own hydro-electric system.
JOHN OXLEY LIBRARY

Left: inspiration could spring from the oddest sources: this fibro-clad slice of Venice, built by Mr and Mrs G.L. Hunt in 1933, was inspired by the backdrop to a production of 'The Gondoliers'.
AUSTRALIAN HOME BEAUTIFUL 1 MAR 1934

'Modern as Tomorrow's Milk' 1940-1960

Whether you stand or sit to iron that monumental pile of shirts, keep your posture good. It not only helps your figure, but saves energy, too. You don't want to be a dutiful, weary wreck when your man comes home, and he doesn't want to hear what a hard day you had; your job's to cluck-cluck sympathetically about his.

Australian House & Garden March 1949

WHEN THE WAR WAS OVER, THE MEN RETURNED TO the jobs the women had been doing in their absence. The women returned reluctantly to the ironing and rehearsed clucking noises for their men to come home to. The only problem was that there weren't enough homes.

During the Great Depression of the 1930s building virtually ceased although the population continued to grow at its usual pace. This meant that even in 1939 the demand for houses was far greater than the supply:

The housing shortage got worse and worse, not only in the metropolis, but also in the country; this was the condition of affairs when the Second World War opened in 1939. Building did not immediately stop, but slowed down seriously; we all thought we should be able to carry on as had been the case in 1914-18. This was not to be! Supplies of materials and labour were required for war purposes and private building ceased unless a permit was granted, and that was only the case where the building was concerned with the war effort. Young architects, builders, and tradesmen all enlisted in the forces, or if not physically fit took government jobs.[1]

By 1945 there was a shortfall of roughly 400 000 homes and no stockpile of materials with which to build them. The scarcity led to a dramatic increase in the cost of houses and building materials; rationing began, and the size of houses was limited to 92 square metres in some cases, 111 square metres in others.

The house Donna Winchester designed is a typical example. While her fiancé Tom served in the navy, Donna dutifully prepared herself for his

QUEENSLAND HOUSING COMMISSION.
DESIGN N° 180.   AREA 1058 sq.ft

Left: houses were in short supply at the end of World War II — 400 000 homemakers were looking for homes. State governments stepped in with basic, but habitable, designs.
QLD HOUSING COMMISSION

Facing page
'Happy the husband who enjoys the restful atmosphere of an easily run home. Happy the wife who can run such a home — whose day is not a weary round of chores, who can find time to relax, see her friends and think of herself. The English Electric company has helped make this possible in homes everywhere.'
AUSTRALIAN WOMEN'S WEEKLY 14 APRIL 1951

Above: a returned soldier's first home in the Northern Territory, 1946, consists of little more than curved corrugated iron from water tanks and ex-army canvas tarpaulins. JIM BROWN

Right: even house designs that were no more than narrow-eaved weather-board boxes with windows and a token brick chimney attracted great interest in the home-starved of 1945. PROMOTION AUSTRALIA

return by taking a course called 'Marriage and the Home'. Students were required to draw a plan of the dream home in which they would while away their years of wedded bliss:

So with twelve hundred square feet of floor space to spend, I immediately squandered half of it on a living-room. Then when I began to add up the reasons for my extravagance, I decided it wasn't an extravagance. First of all, the family could be together without crowding. The living-room would be like my great-grandmother's living-room, in which everything happened. One wall would open out onto a garden in which anything else that cared to would happen. In such a big, friendly, indoor-outdoor room everyone would be on good terms. No one can sulk long in a light, friendly room. There would be sulking rooms, but they would be highly restricted and definitely not inviting.

I had only six hundred square feet left, and out of that had to come three bedrooms. They were small, naturally, but I opened each one with sliding glass onto a little intimate garden, one separated from the others with shrubs.

The kitchen would be compact and U-shaped. What is more intimidating than a large kitchen? It leads to six-layer cakes that would ruin my figure and the children's teeth. But I determined that I would not go without a single cupboard that could possibly be squeezed in over the sink, under the sink, all around the walls, anywhere. And they must have doors that slide up, and are incapable of injuring my head. Then I remembered I would not have to stoop, anyway. Everything would be at my level. If a kitchen was a laboratory, it could well be opened up to the living-room so the chief technician could keep in touch with her family... so I opened up part of the kitchen wall and put in a counter. The laundry, hall and bathroom used up my last six hundred feet.

All this seems ages ago; actually it was 1945. All

The Beaufort house, a prefabricated home designed by Arthur Baldwinson, was mass-produced by the same factory that had built Beaufort bombers in war time.
AUSTRALIAN ARCHIVES

187

Above: 'Masonite could easily obsess the mind of the modern fighting man' reads the copy of this 1942 advertisement. Made from sugarcane fibre, Masonite was everywhere during World War II. *AUSTRALIAN WOMEN'S WEEKLY* 3 MAY 1942

Right: with a friend, Henry Hitchcock, Tom and Donna Winchester built the 112-square-metre dream home Donna had planned while Tom was serving in the Navy. *AUSTRALIAN HOUSE & GARDEN* FEB 1949

at once Tom came home from the Navy, and two days later we were married. We went to live with his family. Then his father gave us a piece of land to build on, and it was at this point that I fished out my old plan.[2]

After a few alterations to the design, Donna and Tom began building the house themselves, completing it in four months at a cost of £1600.

The Winchesters were fortunate they built immediately after the war. The situation would get worse before it got better. In an article called 'When Will We All Have Homes?' published three years later in *Australian Home Beautiful*, Laurie Whitehead wrote:

The present completion rate of new dwellings (it takes not less than six months and more often a year to complete the average villa) is 'braked' down to the supply of materials. Until materials are in freer supply, therefore, no improvement in the completion rate can be expected.

There is no unemployment in any of the basic off-site or on-site building trades — in fact, there is still a grave shortage of labor and the intake of new hands is infinitesimal. So where are the materials to come from?

Outside of the application of atomic power or some remarkable improvement in production techniques, the prospect of increasing the supply of materials for housing appears grimmer than a Boris Karloff film.

Lacking bold planning, adequate supplies of such important items as coal to fire the brick and tile kilns, steel to make the roofing and spouting, ships to transport the supplies from one State to another, labor to dig and mould and shape and use the materials . . . it looks as if this country could muddle along with a housing problem for the next 20, 30 or 50 years.

Paradoxically, builders faced with an unquestioned demand for a quarter of a million houses in the next four years, now fear a slump!

Prices up to stratosphere levels are way past the reach of between 85 and 90 per cent of people who have the land, a set of plans — and no ready cash to

A second generation of Diggers sets out to build homes fit for heroes: members of the 2/28 Battalion Association Housing Scheme work at Kalgoorlie, SA, in 1947.
BATTYE LIBRARY

bridge the gap between housing advances and actual costs.[3]

The result was that house plans were pared down to the very minimum necessary for comfortable shelter. Dining and living rooms were amalgamated, and sometimes the dining area was reduced to an alcove adjoining the kitchen; entrance halls were eliminated in favour of direct entry into the living room; while built-in wardrobes and cupboards saved space and money. Efficiency was a high priority.

Some small house architects such as Leonard Bullen suggested building a core, then working gradually out from it. In his 1949 booklet, *Selected Home Designs Planned for Additions*, he wrote with questionable prose but undeniable common sense:

Under post-war conditions, when the prospective home-owner usually finds it impossible to build his house as large as he would like to build it, he may decide to build a smaller house with a view to enlarging it later. Often he begins with a nucleus of two or three rooms and adds to it as he buys the necessary materials.[4]

Above: founded by Adelaide baker George Palmer in 1946, the South Australian Home Builder's Club swapped labour for expertise in building. The concrete blocks for this, the Palmers' house, were all made by George and his wife.
GEORGE PALMER

Right: shortages encouraged fresh approaches in the late 1940s: in 1949 workmen took only five hours to pour concrete into the formwork of this five-roomed Canberra house.

For many the only solution was to build for themselves, helped by their mates and a book or two. The most popular of these was a step-by-step manual called, simply, *Build Your Own Home*, published by a group called the Home Builder's Advisory in Sydney. Its tone was encouraging:

The man who wants a home urgently and is not prepared to wait till Doomsday for it, will start right in to solve the problem for himself. Now! And he'll SOLVE it!

Can you mix concrete? Of course, you can! Can you read a level? Of course! Can you drive a nail? Certainly! Well, go to it! Within twelve months — assuming you have a block of land — you and your family can move into the first completed part of the house.

No doubt you will have to fight like Hell for some of the materials you want, but nobody gets a home easily these days. This factor, however, will not deter the man who is resolved to get a home around him and his family.[5]

One unique experiment was the South Australian Home Builder's Club, a co-operative founded by George Palmer, an Adelaide baker, in 1946. Although the initial membership was composed mainly of ex-servicemen, it was open to anyone who wanted to join. The club worked on the principle of labour barter, with each member entering into a legal undertaking to repay with his own labour the number of man-hours that were put into his own house. George Palmer, still living in the home he built in Adelaide, reminisced:

The Club had a wide range of trades and services all available in exchange for labour. You could have your plans done by the architects and draftsmen, then there was a foreman who would work in with the owner and organize the trade gangs — concretors, brick or blockmakers, stone or bricklayers, carpenters, plumbers, electricians, plasterers, tilers — we had them all.

Now, a new chum to the building game would not have the same value to a builder as a tradesman so a system was worked out whereby tradesmen received extra time in return for their skills, usually about 2 hours per day.

The great thing was that you didn't need much money to get started.[6]

The work was consistent and demanding, but there also was equality and companionship: 'Everyone worked every weekend, women and men together. It was a very friendly atmosphere, a communal affair — like working on a kibbutz. We all looked forward to it.'[7] Over a fourteen-year period the Club built 300 homes with substantial savings for those involved.

Another, similar scheme was started by Broken Hill Proprietary Limited (BHP):

Up at Port Pirie, the Broken Hill Associated Smelters are helping amateurs to build their own homes, and the local publicans are not seeing as much of that lead bonus as they did once.

There was the case of Kitty Bowhan, a blonde theatre usherette in the dusty town, who changed from glamour to grease every weekend to help her boyfriend and others build a house. Clad in her dirty overalls, Kitty manned the home-made automatic concrete mixer driven by an old motorcycle engine. Apart from these co-operative efforts, there are dozens of married couples who do the whole construction by themselves.[8]

The familiar building materials were preferred — brick, concrete brick, timber, and fibro — but it was quickly realised by some that natural materials such as earth and stone were not only free but freely available, and not subject to rationing. At Warrandyte, Victoria, for example, Russian-born artist Danila Vassilieff built his unusual house out of massive blocks of stone he quarried himself. Beginning in 1940 on a steeply sloping site, Vassilieff blasted a section out of the hill to expose a wall of solid stone which was to be the anchor and inner wall of his house. Then he went to work on the hill opposite with gelignite, splitting huge rocks which were rolled into the creek below before being hauled up to the house site by Vassilieff's homemade crane:

A nostalgic attachment to the nineteenth century pervades many of the owner-built homes of the 1950s, such as the stone-and-timber house built by artist and sculptor Danila Vassilieff.
JOHN ARCHER

The mammoth walls of the living room, fireplace, kitchen, and shower recess were built out from the natural wall, Vassilieff himself manhandling the rocks and buttering them into place. These walls were pierced with small unmatched windows (salvaged from the bushfires or from Whelan the Wrecker) at the level of the ground outside, so that hens, geese, and sunflowers would peer in at eye level. Finally, massive timber logs, felled from the bush and manoeuvred down the hill from above the construction, were rolled across the top of the waiting walls to form the roof.

Built into and out of the ground, this phenomenal abode was in harmony with and, like the earth colours in his paintings, almost indistinguishable from the environment. It expanded almost continuously, growing upwards by way of a staircase carved out of the rock, in response to need and the availability of materials until, in 1946, as the coup de grace he crowned it with a cable tram. The house was derived from the soil, according to the time-honoured Russian custom, though not, in this case, the clay used in his birthplace. For this reason he called it 'Stonygrad': literally, stony place.[9]

At nearby Eltham Justus Jorgensen was putting the finishing touches to the unique complex of buildings he had named 'Monsalvat' after the castle of the Knights of the Holy Grail. It wasn't the first earth building in Eltham by any means. A mud-brick house built by Charles Souter in the 1850s is still in use today, and many other old mud huts remain in the district, but the technique had not been used for many years.

Helped by students and friends, Jorgensen built a cottage with a living room, a bathroom and an attic. Roofing slates were donated by friends; recycled firebricks were used for the floor; window, doors and a cast iron staircase were bought cheaply from a building demolisher's yard.

When finished the building was 79.5 square metres in area, which the local building inspector said was not big enough. Jorgensen agreed to add a bit to it. Several of his students liked the place, so he suggested they build some living quarters using mud brick. A reef of mudstone was found and work started on the Great Hall, an immense Gothic building. The community began to cover a considerable area, and to attract the attention of like-minded people who were interested in helping.

Jorgensen's architecture style was French pro-vincial in character, but it wasn't just the design of his buildings that was unusual. He and his friends were master scavengers of building materials and, at that time, Melbourne provided an excellent source of supply. In the rush to the modern, many fine old buildings were being demolished and a number of them ended up (in part, at least) at Monsalvat. Circular iron staircases, stained-glass and leadlight windows, enormous timber beams, carved stonework; and even, for the floor of the Great Hall, the weathered slabs of slate that once were the cobblestones of Collins Street. Recycled materials were combined with mud brick, rammed earth and stone to produce buildings that looked as though they had been there for centuries.

Many people felt sufficiently stimulated by what they saw at Monsalvat to build their own

Justus Jorgensen, who like many European settlers before him retained a certain nostalgia for the Old Country, built a collection of mud-brick mediaeval buildings near Eltham, Vic; his master-piece, Monsalvat, is in the background.
SIGMUND JORGENSEN

homes out of the same materials. One was Clifton Pugh, who bought land with some friends and built a pioneer style hut in 1951:

I knew nothing whatever about building — I'd never lifted a hammer in my life, but, as I walked all around the area, I found lots of little wattle and daub houses which still survived from the gold mining period of the 1860s and 70s. This was one of the first gold areas in Victoria, and here were all these places still standing.

It wasn't very difficult to work out how they were built — you just had to look at them closely. They were only saplings nailed on to bush poles and plastered with mud. It looked simple and cheap and attractive

So my first building was wattle and daub and it's still there in the centre of the existing house — well, all the original posts and some of the walls. I put the posts straight into the ground. I couldn't go any deeper than 225 mm because under here is a solid quartz reef. When I hit that I stopped.

Initially the first place was about 6 metres by 4 metres with a dirt floor and a large fireplace. I built the whole thing in 12 days and moved in.[10]

Monsalvat also made a lasting impression on a bank clerk and part-time builder named Alistair Knox. By 1950 Knox had designed and built eight houses using mud brick, which he felt was perfect as a material because it gave the house a unity with the site. Knox was enthusiastic about developing an Australian style of architecture using earth as the medium. His interview with *Australian Home Beautiful* in January 1953 was called 'He Crusades for Mud':

With earth building, beauty can be expressed simply: natural and honest treatment of the walls so that they retain some of the primeval quality of earth; a true sense of topography through the proper handling of the site; a strong sense of shelter by deft use of the thick walls so that they cast deep shadows at the reveals; the use of simple masses, moulded or curved walls to show the pliancy of the medium; proportions that are unpretentious and fundamental, not frivolous.

No material is more responsive to human expression than mud, provided the initial objectives are not lost sight of — retention of its primeval character, and absolute avoidance of nonsense.

Knox was not only poetic, he was extremely persuasive. Even conservative bodies such as the Queensland Housing Commission produced a book on mud-brick construction and built two demonstration earth houses in Brisbane.

Melbourne truck driver Jack Ross had always wanted to build a house with these mud bricks he had heard so much about, until one day he saw some ex-Army rocket boxes for sale at five shillings each. He realised the solidly made hardwood cases would make ideal units for building walls:

Of course as soon as I saw them I saw mud bricks except they were wooden bricks. I couldn't understand why everyone couldn't see immediately that you could build a house out of them. When I was a little boy I used to build houses with wooden blocks so it registered immediately. I went down to the Council and asked if they'd let me build a house out of boxes. They said, 'Oh no!' I asked them if I could bring a box in for them to look at. The Engineer was a fair sort of a bloke and he agreed to think about it. So I brought a box back and as soon as he saw it, he said, 'Okay, you can build what you like out of those'.

So we scrapped the mud brick idea for the studio and used the boxes.

We poured the concrete slab for the floor. It took a week and I worked like a horse. Around the perimeter I set bolts in the concrete then we bolted the first course of boxes to the slab. After that we laid them in bonded courses just as you'd lay bricks. Here and there we'd leave a box out of the wall and these cavities would be cupboards and bookshelves.

It was so quick that we put the walls of the first storey up in a day. I thought, this is no good. I wanted something to do, so I put another storey on top of it. That went up quickly too although it was

more conventional material, timber lined with bondwood from old tractor crates.

Then I thought, 'Dammit, I'll build another one on top of that!' I'd got a building permit for a one-storey building and I thought, 'I won't bother the council — after all I'm just extending upwards'. When the shire engineer finally came to see it he checked it over and gave it the okay anyway.[11]

Jack Ross's unconventional solution to the shortage of building materials passed unnoticed. However, one postwar Australian innovation that did come to stay was brick veneer.

Although it was developed much earlier, the concept was refined and improved by postwar builders trying to stretch their ration of bricks as far as possible. A brick veneer is essentially a timber-framed house sheeted with brick instead of weatherboard. The load-bearing frame is supported by brick foundations which also provide support for the external brick skin. In addition to economy, the speed and versatility of brick veneer

ensured its continued success.

Status was important, too. Because it was cheap and relatively available, timber was frowned on in many areas as the building material for those who could afford no better. Brick was definitely the symbol of material success in the suburban hierarchy, and brick veneer offered a cut-price way to achieve it.

In terms of design, it was important not to be too radical on one hand, nor too old-fashioned on the other. The triple-fronted style with square corners (or rounded corners for the adventurous) emerged as the most acceptable. So began the saga of the celebrated triple-fronted brick veneer (in red or cream) which would eventually become the symbol of suburban conformity and security.

Inside, the illusion continued. The furniture was also covered with veneer, this time of Queensland walnut or silky oak, to conceal the hardwood beneath. Lounge suites, bulky and overstuffed, were upholstered with patterned Genoa velvet, while kitchen cabinets and sideboards were fitted with mass-produced leadlight doors. In 1945 one

With few exceptions, the postwar rule was that the more expensive the house, the more conservative its design. These Perth houses owed more to pre-war days than to the architectural fashions of the 1940s and 1950s.
BATTYE LIBRARY

195

Above: like the identical terraces of the 1890s, identical spec-built houses mushroomed in every Australian city as postwar demand exceeded most home-buyers' ability — and desire — to obtain individual designs.
AUSTRALIAN ARCHIVES

Left: masonite panels occupy window frames until the owners of this West Australian house can afford glazing to complement its handsome and streamlined stuccoed chimney.
AUSTRALIAN ARCHIVES

Above: bargain furnishings from the Pitt Street, Sydney, firm of J.A. Booth. In 1945, the new homeowner could purchase three complete rooms of 'comfortable solid' furniture for £75.

purveyor of such 'exclusive ... furniture', J.A. Booth of Pitt Street, Sydney, offered customers the exciting possibility of filling four rooms with the 'finest modern suites available' for only £100.

Queensland author David Malouf, in *12 Edmonstone Street*, describes a typical lounge room and speculates on the meaning of its existence:

Carefully composed and grandly furnished, with a Genoa-velvet lounge suite, sideboards with barley-sugar legs and little glass-topped occasional tables, its three sash windows hung with curtains of a dusky-pink colour, with ropes and tassels of gold, our Front Room is a show place.

Beside each of the three Genoa-velvet lounge-chairs is a smoker's stand, polished brass with a cut-glass bowl. In one, the column is plain but the tray is embossed at the rim with lilies; the others, a pair, have plain trays but the columns are liquor-ice-twists. On the bow-fronted sideboard, which

matches a dining-table and chairs, is an array of glassware, all Webb and Corbett crystal: a whisky set with straight-sided glasses and a square decanter, a sherry set with stemmed glasses and a decanter like a giant teardrop, and a silver cock-tail-shaker with swizzle sticks whose tops represent the suits in a pack of cards. All these objects, the three smoker's stands, the drinking sets, the cock-tail-shaker, are wedding presents; their display is obligatory. But they are also clues I decide, after long thought, to what our Front Room has been set up for and why we are forbidden to go there.

My parents do not smoke or drink, and my mother, though a passionate and daring bridge-player, who will go no trumps on nothing, is dead set against all forms of gambling.

Our Front Room is a warning, richly put, against easy pleasures and the dangers of 'the social life'. The instruments of smoking and drinking are made visible, displayed and kept in a state of awful

Before television became the opiate of the suburbs, families used their living rooms for conversation, reading to children, or keeping up with the latest radio serial.
AUSTRALIAN ARCHIVES

Postwar austerity became its own style, epitomised by clean design and a minimum of frills (no window pelmets, flat ceilings, and simple light fittings). Even so, the consumers' urge to display their wealth found satisfaction in overstuffed, styleless furniture and as many appliances as possible.
BOTTOM LEFT:
BATTYE LIBRARY

glitter; but only to demonstrate their attractiveness, and to show how firmly, in this house, they are resisted. [12]

After the drab uniformity of wartime paint, colour returned in a blaze of a glory, transforming lounge rooms, dining rooms and kitchens with garish blues, reds and oranges. Paint companies were a never-ending source of inspiration on 'daring colour schemes to brighten up your life'. Even the hipped roof was often covered with the latest cement tiles, coloured green, grey, blue or yellow, and sometimes artfully arranged in spotted or diagonal patterns. The garden reflected this geometry, with straight concrete paths bisecting neat beds containing disciplined rows of flowers and carefully pruned shrubs.

By 1951 the shortage of houses and building materials was becoming less of a problem, despite the hundreds of thousands of immigrants from Europe who helped to increase the demand. One hundred and seventy thousand arrived in 1950

alone; they brought with them new ideas and skills which would eventually change many of the patterns of Australian culture.

One immigrant from Canada was the young Vienna-born architect Harry Seidler, who decided Australia was now ready for something completely different. At Turramurra, then on the outskirts of Sydney, he built a flat-roofed 'machine for living' — a box with large picture windows and an unconventional cantilevered concrete slab floor supported by stone walls and pipe columns.

Home Beautiful was impressed. In 'Sydney Showpiece' (February 1951), Nora Cooper announced:

Houses of a style new to Australia are appearing on Sydney's North Shore. One is at Turramurra, in wild country ...

The style is still novel in Europe and America, and the architect, a Canadian, Harry Seidler, believes that Australians will accept the new style now they can see houses that have been built here.

Cantilever construction makes the utmost use of

Probably the most famous twentieth-century house in Australia, the Turramurra, NSW, home Harry Seidler designed for his parents resonated with architectural purity; fashionable detail was restricted to cerebral linear arrangements.
MAX DUPAIN

199

Few of Australia's architects have been as influential as Harry Seidler. His uncompromisingly hard-edged houses inspired a totally new approach to design — exemplified by this cantilevered house from Ancher, Mortlock and Woolley in 1953.
NEW AUSTRALIAN HOME

site and outlook. Glass walls diffuse daylight through living areas shaped to suit family needs, providing play and study space for children without interfering with grown-ups.

Inside wall partitions are reduced to a minimum, creating a feeling of space and restful vistas while preserving the entity of sections for dining, study or entertainment. Garden outlets are plentiful and sliding sections do away with the noise of banging doors. Concealed lighting and softly-blended colors in every part of the house encourage relaxation and make housework pleasant.

In these light engineering structures, foundation work is reduced to a minimum. The whole house may be raised from the ground on what appear to be the slenderest supports, setting free valuable

outdoor living space beneath.

The Modern house had arrived, though it was some time before it was made to feel welcome.

One of the innovations of the Modern house was the emphasis on indoor-outdoor living, and a dawning appreciation of the Australian environment:

More and more the trend is to open the walls of the contemporary house to the great outdoors. This is particularly so in the more rural areas now being developed. Many building lots have enchanting views of water or beaches, some have mountains or perhaps a less expansive view of gum trees and wild flora in its natural state.[13]

Above: 'Australians . . . like to take refreshments out of doors and cultivate neat gardens' reads the caption to this promotional photograph aimed at attracting houseproud immigrants. PROMOTION AUSTRALIA

Left: the vacation lifestyle of the late 1950s: the Australian outdoors could be enjoyed from the proto-Scandinavian lines of a wooden deck and the comfort of chrome and vinyl furniture. PROMOTION AUSTRALIA

Harry Seidler's work has been imitated badly in hundreds of houses, yet his own designs retain a distinctive air of tension between the curves of nature and the right angles of the building.
NEW AUSTRALIAN HOME

In 1952 a house in the Seidler mode at Avalon featured:

a lack of strict division between various areas or 'rooms' and also the apparent elimination of a line of demarkation between the actual house and its surroundings. This is produced by patio paving which continues indoors through unbroken glass and by wide eaves projections which virtually form verandahs.

Warwick Kells has used an unusual method of construction. The roof is of flat concrete. This is supported by two slab-like stone walls and slender pipe columns. The remainder of the walls and partitions are filled in beneath this self-supporting frame. These walls are glass and timber. The glass walls, which stretch from floor to ceiling of the

living sections, are completely without a frame — the glass slides on ball bearings in a track.[14]

The window wall was an integral part of this new approach to life. It simplified construction and lowered its cost at the same time as it let in light and air. This concept appealed to the Melbourne architect and author Robin Boyd. A committed Functionalist since the 1930s, Boyd helped establish the Stegbar company in order to manufacture the window wall and other innovative designs suitable for the sort of house he felt appropriate.

Peter McIntyre, friend, companion and fellow architect, worked with Boyd during those years:

Boyd wanted to change the Australian house, and

Above: designed and built primarily as an intellectual exercise, this Frankston, Vic, house by Roy Grounds nevertheless inspired architects and owner-builders with its fresh ideas.
NEW AUSTRALIAN HOME

Left: in the context of the new architecture of the 1950s and 1960s, architect Kenneth McDonald may have been justified in writing that his butterfly-roofed house represented a 'harmony between the environment and the well-designed house'.
NEW AUSTRALIAN HOME

In a tropical variation on the curtain wall so beloved by the commercial architects of the 1960s, the walls of this Northern Territory house are almost entirely louvred.
AUSTRALIAN ARCHIVES

specifically he wanted to bring logic and honesty back into our buildings. If a block of land faced west, for instance, why have the living room and the main bedroom facing the street when these would become unbearably hot by nightfall. Boyd wanted to site the house so that it broke with the conventions of the time.

Honest expression of materials was another platform. If there was a piece of timber used or a concrete wall, he wanted this exposed for what it was.

The vast majority of Australians were quite happy following the established conventions, so Boyd set out deliberately to alter public opinion. He started the Age Small Homes Service where good architecturally designed houses were offered to the public for the nominal sum of £5. This brought architectural work within the purchasing power of people on average incomes — a critical point when endeavouring to influence the public.[15]

Boyd went even further than this. In conjunction with McIntyre and several other like-minded architects he designed a series of Modern houses in some of the new bayside suburbs of Melbourne;

they were marketed as 'Peninsula Homes'. Architect Norman Day recalls:

They were promoting a new open lifestyle — and the people believed in it wholeheartedly. The architects themselves were politically, morally and philosophically of the left leaning, so they felt that they should direct their energy towards the people, not the landed gentry.[16]

It proved to be one of the rare instances in Australia's history when the aspirations of avant-garde architects and those of the general public were united. The Peninsula Homes were an incredible success and people crowded to look ... and buy.

Modern homes needed modern furniture, and modern retailers were quick to seize the opportunity to supply it. Open planning eliminated heavy furniture; the new look was spare, light and economical. Vinyl-covered chairs with frames of thin black-painted iron, chrome chairs and tables with Laminex tops, and Vynex-covered lounges in mottled colours replaced the walnut veneer and Genoa velvet.

By the late 1950s a new descriptive adjective had

arrived. Art, music, furniture and architecture were now Contemporary, to distinguish them from Modern, which was already five years old — built-in obsolescence had been extended to the vocabulary. This was not lost on some observers. Humorist Cyril Pearl, in a satirical work called *So You Want to Buy a House*, has one character delivering a paper on Contemporary architecture:

What do we mean by 'contemporary'? The word, in its architectural context, derives from 'con', an abbreviation of 'confidence-trick', and 'temporary', meaning temporary. In short, comrades, it's a swindle that won't last.

A contemporary house is one that was put up yesterday, is put up with today, and will be ka-put tomorrow. It is obsolete before the gum on the back of the duty-stamp on the front of the mortgage is dry. Obsolescence is a built-in feature like the broom-cupboard. This is economically important. It keeps the wheels of industry turning on an even keel . . .

It has been said that 'contemporary' is a word to conjure with. If you're no good at conjuring, it's a word to keep your eye on.

Today, any house that looks like a packing-case with glass where the wood should be, or that is stuck up on sticks like a Tahitian fisherman's hut or a New Guinea cannibal's tree-house, is 100 per cent contemporary, and as modern as tomorrow's milk . . .

Of course . . . contemporary design has some

Nothing more than glass divides interior from exterior in this relentlessly rectilinear 'contemporary' dwelling, whose right angles are broken only by a suitably spiky potted plant.

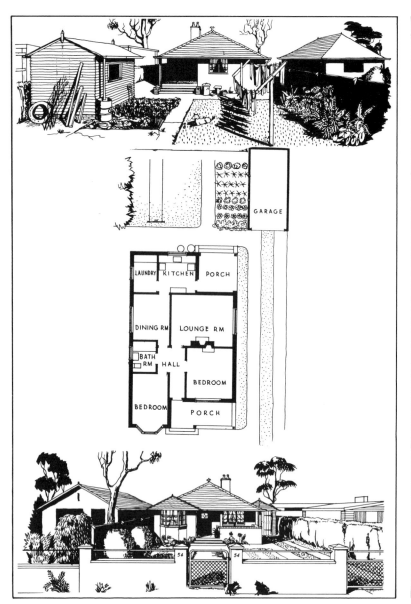

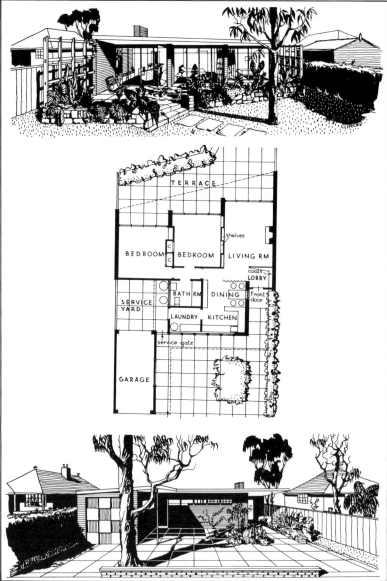

Much has been gained as the 1920s home evolves into the rational house of 1950, although most contact with the natural world has been lost as backyard becomes paved terrace.
AUSTRALIAN HOUSE & GARDEN SEPT 1950

advantages. One is its very great flexibility. You draw up your plans, pocket your fee, and leave your client to decide what to do with the building when it's finished. He can sell it as a fashionable home, a police-station, a bank, a cats' hospital, a two-up school, a garage or a fertiliser-factory — according to the state of the market — since they all look the same.

In my country, the most popular thing in the contemporary home is the window-wall. This is a generously proportioned slab of glass replacing the old-fashioned wall that you couldn't see through. If you look through your generously-proportioned window-wall, you can enjoy the sight of your neighbours enjoying the sight of you through their generously-proportioned window-wall as you enjoy the sight of them through your generously-proportioned window-wall enjoying the sight of you through their generously-proportioned window-wall as you enjoy the sight of them . . .

The window-wall also has economic importance. As one of our greatest poets has written:

People who live in glass houses
Need trouses.

For this reason, the glass wall has been endorsed by the joint executives of the Trouser-Makers' and Textile-Workers' Unions of Australasia.[17]

Pearl went on to point out that for people who were mixed up aesthetically there was a compromise, the semi-contemporary home; while for schizophrenics, split level homes had possibilities.

In 1956, the Contemporary living room was suddenly altered. Chairs that once faced each other across a kidney-shaped coffee table were now rearranged so that everyone could look at the new arrival in the corner. Television had reached Australia.

It took people a while to adjust to the new way of life. *House & Garden* offered some helpful advice on 'How to Rearrange Rooms for TV':

Now that TV is firmly established in Australia and we have had time to learn from experience its influence on home planning, let's give some thought

WINDSOR
3 - piece unit suite
OVER ONE FOOT DEEP
LUXURY **TV** COMFORT

to re-arranging its place in the room . . .

Whichever arrangement suits your kind of living, the set should always be placed for viewing where the whole family can see without eye strain and discomfort. Too, there should be no glare from the screen. You'll know by now how important it is to have a background lamp on and enough seating units of the soft lounging type to make viewing physically relaxing as well as entertaining! And a television set usually means more entertaining at home, more informal visits, so that guests must be catered for easily.[18]

The corner TV lounge appeared. 'It's like floating on air . . . night after night . . . year after year . . . truly luxurious TV relaxation,' promised the manufacturers of the Windsor suite, 'Delightfully upholstered in uncut moquette or bouclé.'

Throughout suburban Australia, families relaxed with a bag of Minties in front of the evening news and shows such as Bob Dyer's 'Pick-a-Box'. One of the early television programmes produced by Hector Crawford was a series in which Robin Boyd and Peter McIntyre continued their crusade for logic in housing. Their persistence would be rewarded in the decades to come.

As bare of decoration as a church pew — though considerably more comfortable — the TV lounge was carefully positioned to face Australia's brand new black-and-white electronic altar.

'Inside the Illusion' 1960-1988

*The universal visual art, the art of shaping the human environment,
is an intellectual, ethical, and emotional exercise as well as a means of expression.
It involves the strange sort of possessive love with which people have always
regarded their shelters. The Australian ugliness begins with fear of reality,
denial of the need for the everyday environment to reflect the heart
of the human problem, satisfaction with veneer
and cosmetic effects.*

Robin Boyd *The Australian Ugliness*

THE TYPICAL CONTEMPORARY HOME AS IT EMERGED in the early 1960s had an L-shaped open plan with a skillion roof and the external walls boldly finished in bright colours. The attached carport, a flat roof supported by ornamental black iron poles, displayed a two-tone Holden.

Display was also important in the interior of the house; and if you didn't have something special to show off, you created it. In the Scarf home on Sydney's North Shore, this was a colourful marble foyer:

many people might long for a marble entrance to their home and do nothing about it; but the Scarfs actually saw to it that they had one.

It extends from the front porch into the entrance hall and is made from marble offcuts, in colors ranging from green to various shades of amber and off-white; Mr Scarf himself helped a stonemason lay and set the chips in cement and pebble.[1]

For those who didn't want to go to so much trouble there was the feature wall. This could be covered with an eye-catching wallpaper — a larger-than-life photographic mural of Germany's Black Forest in autumn, for example — or a lining of vertical boards coated with Estapol, a clear plastic gloss paint which produced a bright 'natural' finish like timber in aspic.

Robin Boyd called the phenomenon 'Featurism' and, in *The Australian Ugliness*, painted a witty but accurate picture of the Featurist family room:

The room's main feature is not really the feature wall in the yellow vertical v-jointed Pinus Insignus boards, nor the featured fireplace faced with autumnal stone veneer, nor the vinyl tiled floor in marbled grey with feature tiles of red and yellow let in at random, nor the lettuce-green Dunlopillo convertible daybed set before the Queensland Maple television receiver, nor any of the house-wifely features hung on the walls; nor the floor-stand ash-tray in chromium and antique-ivory, nor even the glass aquarium on the wrought-iron stand under the window. The real feature of the room is the tea table, groaning with all kinds of good foods set in a plastic dream. The table top features hard laminated plastic in a pattern of pinks resembling the Aurora Australis. The table mats are a lace-work of soft plastic, the red roses in the central bowl are a softer plastic, the pepper and salt shakers are the hardest of all. And, soft or hard, all this plastic is featured in the most vivid primary pillar-box red, butter yellow, sky blue, pea green, innocent of any idea of secondary or tertiary tints, and all strikingly prominent against the pale, hot pastel tints of the flat plastic paint on the walls; all vibrating like a chromatrope beneath the econom-ical brilliance of the fluorescent tubes on the ceiling. The main feature of the feature window is immediately apparent: the venetian blinds featured in a pastel tint. But look again and discover that this is more than one tint; every slat of the blinds is a different pastel hue. And if you look more closely

Facing page
'Modern' was no longer enough to describe the house of the 1960s; 'contemporary' sounded more up-to-date, more suited to the minimalist features of this split-level brick house, carport, tidy garden and Pope mower.
AUSTRALIAN ARCHIVES

The 1960s saw the first tentative attempts to reintroduce the kitchen as the social centre of the house. A servery could overcome poor design — and reduce the isolation of the cook.

still you may discover, if this is a very up-to-date house, that every aluminium blade of the blind carries a printed pattern, perhaps of tiny animals done in aboriginal style. Everywhere, the closer you look the more features you see, as in the old novelty picture of a man holding a portrait of himself holding a portrait of himself holding a portrait of himself, until the artist's and the viewer's eyesight fails.[2]

Changes were taking place, however. The open plan began to fall from favour as people could now afford to pay for additional space. Dens and rumpus rooms appeared. The Scarf home had a floor plan that would have been typical thirty years earlier; now it was considered 'adventurous' and 'exciting':

Mrs Scarf was determined, for instance, not to have an 'open plan' for the living areas. In a previous 'open plan' home she had found it impractical with three young daughters to cope with and clear up after. She now has four daughters and has found in her new house that a conventional hallway, with a door at centre that divides the house into almost equal halves of living and sleeping areas, has resulted in less confusion and easier management for both adults and children.

Replacing a large living/dining area is a den for television, reading and entertaining. Its color scheme — red and black with off-white accents! The walls are lined with Masonite's silver birch Seadrift and this is again repeated on doors of the bookshelf cabinet. Carpet and divan are red, curtains red and white striped. Exposed timber beams painted black are striking.

Across the hallway from the den is the dining room, large and comfortable and floored in practical Vinyl tiles. The dining room has access to the

kitchen through the large open hatchway.[3]

Kitchens grew larger and often included island bench tops copied from American magazines:

The kitchen itself is a sun-filled room with its warm timber tones and lemon-yellow bench tops tempered by cool green-and-white striped blinds, light-grey Vinyl tiles and a calm, pretty wallpaper. It's a beautifully composed room, with a large area of working benches surrounding the island counter cooking top in the centre of the room, and an abundance of cupboards below counters. Nice touches are the polished copper jelly moulds hung on the wall and an open cupboard for spice jars on the wall covered by a small wooden awning.[4]

Bathrooms were expanded to include a separate toilet, and a shower alcove in addition to the built-in bath. Vanity basins replaced the old fashioned hand-basins and second bathrooms and en-suites started to appear in designs.

The new Ranch style houses of the mid-1960s suburbs had wide low-pitched roofs with walls of rough clinker bricks, Canadian red cedar and/or off-form concrete. Their long rectangular shapes presented a broad frontage to the street, often requiring blocks 25 metres wide. Invariably, a full-length verandah was included with white-painted floor-to-ceiling windows. The two-car garage with roller doors was fitted beneath the main roof.

Although the buildings they produced were far more original, the Sydney School of architects also used natural unpainted materials — clinker brick, rough-sawn timber, and brown quarry tile floors. Many of their houses were built on steeply sloping sites and were stepped down the inclines, creating many different levels. One was Professor R.N.

Laminated-plastic work surfaces, vinyl tiling, and plastic paints made the 1960s kitchen easier to keep clean than its predecessors, even if it was no more imaginative.
PROMOTION AUSTRALIA

In many respects the supremely rational skeletal house — complete with high stumps and broad shady verandahs — of the 1960s was remarkably similar to early settler's homes.
JACK MCNEISH

Johnson's home in the Sydney suburb of Chatswood, built in 1963:

The house was designed to disturb the site as little as possible and it occupies a relatively small part of it. It was thought of as a man-made cliff which might always have been there complementing the site and sustaining its character, uniting with the site at different levels. Meeting the rock shelves with terrace and bridge and touching the tops of the trees with its verandahs.[5]

Not all these architects were men. In 1968 *Australian Home Beautiful* featured the work of several women, among them Judith Brine, who had her own ideas about gender and the new architecture:

If it were left to women architects like Judith Brine, the present-day Australian house would be strong, robust — even cave-like — and relatively unadorned.

Women, she says, subconsciously prefer their houses to be like their ideal men — practical and ruggedly masculine.

It's the men who — idealising the soft, feminine

type of woman — seek to express these qualities in their houses. Hence the frills and 'feminine' touches in the finish and furnishing of the average house . . .

As with most young couples, economy was an over-riding consideration. Both worked on various construction stages and concentrated on simple materials used as 'naturally' as possible — unpainted manganese brick walls internally and externally, natural-finished timbers, corrugated aluminium ceilings ('simply fixed, highly light-reflective and efficient as insulation').

Characteristically, they refused to disguise or try to hide essential structural members purely for the sake of appearance.

Exposed rolled steel joists and massive reinforced concrete beams are seen to be doing their job of supporting the wide expanse of concrete that forms the upper-storey floor.

And, on the underside of that slab, the pattern of the formboards helps to heighten the 'cave-like' atmosphere of the ground-level areas.[6]

Project housing was a marketing concept aimed at the middle and lower income groups. At its best

Above: the Australian dream begins: engagement ring discretely visible, a young wife-to-be inspects the plans for a home that will most likely be mortgaged for decades to come.
PROMOTION AUSTRALIA

Left: efforts to control the spiralling costs of building usually took the form of savings that made life less comfortable for occupants: cheap materials and design shortcuts, such as low chimneys and narrow eaves, were common in the late 1960s.
PROMOTION AUSTRALIA

Ron Tandberg's 1980 comment about the sameness of suburban housing would have been appropriate at any time in the past century, from the terraces of 1880 onwards.
A MANSION OR NO HOUSE

Above: mortgage rates rising faster than incomes meant project housing was the only way most young Australians could realise the dream of home ownership. While some project homes were well designed, most were as unattractive as the Camden.
PROMOTION AUSTRALIA

Right: 'Australians buying a new home ... want space and lots of it' was the judgment of architect-builders Pettit and Sevitt, who won several design awards for their homes and interiors.
PROMOTION AUSTRALIA

it was a sincere attempt to provide well-designed houses at reasonable prices. The Lend Lease Corporation, at its Kingsdene Estate in Carlingford, New South Wales, introduced the idea of project housing within a landscaped environment. The architects who produced the house plans for this development were among the most prestigious of the day: Ken Woolley, Neville Gruzman, Nino Sydney, Towell, Jansen and Rippon, and Harry Seidler. Pettit and Sevitt in Sydney and Merchant Builders in Melbourne also produced high quality, architect-designed plans for their project homes.

One observer in 1967 commented:

In planning for mass housing, the gap between the architects and people still exists. In absolute numbers, the houses designed by architects are increasing every year, but the proportion of architects' houses to the whole of house building may very well be falling.

Some architects think that the cultural upsurge and rising prosperity in this country will correct any downward trend. But whatever the future holds, today's architect-designed houses are for the few and wealthier.

The gap has been narrowed, however, by the commissioning of many architects to design homes for repetition construction by project builders.

These have improved immensely the quality of project houses and widened the field of choice. The practice has also speeded up the rate at which architects' creative ideas, appearing first in custom-designed homes, are being spread through new houses in all price levels.[7]

New estates like Kingsdene, coupled with the demand for larger blocks of land, spread Australian cities over a much broader geographic area than in other countries. The Australian Dream was creating a nightmare:

Australians have always shown a penchant for living in a bungalow of their own surrounded by their own lawn and garden, so that as the land near the centre of the city was taken up they moved further and further out to acquire their own self-contained building block. The result: immense urban spread, huge residential suburbs, long distances between home and work, and public services strained to breaking point. Melbourne, with a

Yours for $24000 in 1971 — a meretricious confusion of bad design, from the 1950s weatherboard gable to the pressed metal awning and the frilly verandah valance, made up the 'Colonial' home.

Adapted largely from Californian models, many 'handmade' houses of the 1970s were reminiscent of early settlers' huts. Skills such as shingle splitting enjoyed a small revival.
JOHN ARCHER

quarter of the population of London, covers an area twice the size. The continuously developed area of Sydney extends over an incredible 600 square miles; public services are so far behind the spreading bungalows and fibro cottages that in 1960 some 360,000 people in the outer suburbs and 124,000 elsewhere — in fact a quarter of the city's population — were without mains sewerage.[8]

When the problems of the moment become too overwhelming, one avenue of escape is into the future. Many 1960s magazines speculated on 'The House of Tomorrow' and its possibilities. Their predictions were often surprisingly accurate:

In 1999 it will take a housewife only two minutes to order, cook and serve the Sunday lunch. The food will be selected by push-button controls from a menu on the electronic screen ordered from the freezer on an automated kitchen console, cooked in a microwave oven, and served on disposable dishes made from powdered plastic in a dishmaker.[9]

The same article predicted shopping by video, to be paid for automatically by computer. All humans had to do was press buttons; the home computer would be the new master of the house:

By far the most revolutionary aspect of the house will be the use of a central computer to control all internal systems. The freedom of design offered by microcircuits — tiny chips no larger than the head of a pin, yet containing an entire circuit — will make possible an electronic complex that will automatically control all lighting, entertainment equipment, appliances and communications gear in a space the size of a contemporary portable radio.[10]

In revolt against the cult of automation was the philosophy of the 'back to the land' movement that began in the early 1970s. Dissatisfied with the pace and style of life in the cities, the high cost of houses, pollution and suburban alienation, some people were attracted by the concept of rural community and small farm self-sufficiency. Their dream became known as the 'alternative lifestyle'.

'Alternative' houses were as varied as their owners, who sometimes looked to other cultures for inspiration. North American Indian tepees, Mongolian yurts, the high-roofed houses of Batak Sumatra and the spare elegant homes of traditional Japan all added a new dimension to our domestic architecture. But the main influence was still from the United States, just as it was in the suburbs.

Books featuring Alternative houses from California and New Mexico sold in their thousands to a generation desperate to escape from conformity and to create their own vision of the world. Craftsmanship and originality were emphasised, rather than fashion or comfort. Materials from the site were preferred where possible, for reasons of economy and visual harmony, and these were augmented with secondhand doors, windows, and fittings recycled from demolished buildings.

The home of Neville Ackland in the Adelaide Hills is one example:

Neville began about 4½ years ago, working on weekends. He made full use of free or cheap local resources — stone lying in the paddocks and in old ruins, sand from the river, railway sleepers, timber poles from a friend's stringy bark forest, 'reject' slate, recycled doors and fittings, and timber off-cuts.

He had little experience in building before he commenced. Neville, now a farmer, has been a woolclasser, social worker, and an antique dealer. And he has ingenuity, imagination, and a belief that it is not necessary to spend vast amounts of money on modern house design, plumbing, electrical appliances, and interior decoration. Hence the stone cottage has no septic tank, no tiled bathroom, no modern kitchen, no electric or gas hot water service, no 240 volt electrical service, and no exhaust fans.

Instead washing water flows to the garden, the bath is set in an interior rockery garden with indoor plants, the refrigerator and stove use bottled L.P. gas, lighting consists of a 12 volt electrical system (with 40 watt globes) connected to the car battery, hot water comes from a wood

217

Revival of craft skills, recycling of materials, and a community-based approach to building and living were features of the 1970s search for new ways. This mud-brick house is in the Moora-Moora community at Healesville, Vic. PROMOTION AUSTRALIA

burning hot water service and the kitchen is part of the total living area centred around a fire-place with mezzanine sleeping and storage areas set at each end of the cottage. Ventilation is provided by two small windows set in the lofty gables above the mezzanines. The windows, when opened, allow the prevailing winds to quickly ventilate the whole house.

The stone cottage has a rustic theme with the stone and concrete walls, and window and door frames made from railway sleepers trimmed with an adze. The roof and ceiling consists of pressed straw panels, insulation material, radiata pine and stringy bark poles trimmed with a draw knife, and good quality corrugated sheeting. The biggest expense was the glass for the windows![11]

The reaction against prevailing materialist values created a novel form of reverse materialism. Where a couple of suburban homeowners would proudly point out that their house had cost all of $100 000, the Alternative family would boast that theirs had cost only $100.

Even among the alternative lifestylers there was considerable competition to see who could build with the smallest cash outlay. One of these buildings was an attic bedroom-studio built by Alistair Knox's son, Macgregor, when he was fifteen:

It is composed of large posts, wattle and daub infills, and attached to the room he was living in. The cost of the house in materials purchased, apart from the glass and the electrical connections, was $7 for some rusty iron. The odd timber and bricks were purchased from odd materials we had lying around the property. In fact the further we have gone the better the results, provided you do it yourself, either by direct work or the exchange of talents with other members within the community.[12]

Alistair Knox, whose practice as a designer of

Some owner-builders sought to make their dwellings so in tune with the environment that they became indistinguishable from it. This ferrocement dome in the bush of northern New South Wales could almost be a lichen-covered boulder.
JOHN ARCHER

219

Leunig

mud-brick homes had grown spectacularly over the years, was a tireless exponent of the virtues of the alternative lifestyle and his book *Living in the Environment* was widely read:

There is seldom a day goes past without some new person discussing with me the idea of earth-wall building. The enquiries come from all sections of society in suburban, semi-rural, and rural living areas, and from those in the lowest through to the highest income brackets. There is a fundamental movement in the hearts of many people to find an alternative to the ticky-tacky and pressed out plastic products that have neither sensuous appeal nor spiritual value. A revulsion has set in against quantity at the price of quality because such things in themselves soon clog and clutter.

The growing premonition that there could be an environmental collapse of nature intensifies the issues in ever increasing circles, and it is this search for genuine simplification of life style that will cause earth to become once again of primary importance as a building medium in the erstwhile sophisticated societies.[13]

By the late 1970s the word 'environment' was almost compulsory at parties, and Environmental architecture became a fashionable style.

The theme of Environmental architecture was integration with the surrounding bush landscape, a concept promoted by Griffin, Walling and others in earlier years. The houses had several recognisable features: many were built on sloping sites, excavated well into the hillside, sometimes so deeply that the rear retaining walls were as high as the eaves, thereby integrating the roofline into the hillside.

The roofs were usually of galvanised iron, coloured to blend with the grey-green of the gums. The soil from the excavation provided the raw material for mud bricks for the walls. Post-and-beam construction using recycled bridge decking, and large-dimension timber for the uprights, simplified the building work.

Internally the mud-brick walls were left in their natural state, complemented by polished brick floors, stained glass, hand-hewn beams, and large open fireplaces. Expansive living areas were often lit by high-set clerestory windows.

Some speculative builders were quick to observe and market this image:

A delightful and really spacious mud brick home with exposed beams, panelled ceilings, etc. Huge living area with open fire and pot belly stove. Excell. kitchen, large pantry, fabulous main bedroom, 20 x 20 plus W.I. robe and en suite. Beautiful windows (some stained glass), quality carps., etc., 2 more bedrooms, plus very large attic type 4th bedr. upstairs. Study with balcony, lge studio, workshop, and CP, pleasant rose and native garden. Filtered pool and many other features. Real value and a new lifestyle at $127,000.[14]

Ron Langman thought $127000 was far too expensive for a new lifestyle, and decided to create his Adelaide house out of sixteen huge (2.5 x 2.5 x 4.2 metre) concrete box culverts. These were assembled — with the aid of a crane — on a concrete raft slab and within four-and-a-half weeks the Langman's 296-square-metre luxury

Above: photographer Ron Langman made use of sixteen concrete box culverts, each 2.5 metres high, 2.5 metres deep and 4.2 metres wide, in the construction of his home.
RON LANGMAN

Above left: this windmill house outside Melbourne was built by a homesick Dutch family and uses wind power to generate some of its electricity.
PROMOTION AUSTRALIA

Left: constructed at Bendigo, Vic, in 1979, this modular triple-dome house incorporates solar space, water and pool heating using an Australian steel solar collector.
PROMOTION AUSTRALIA

Inspired by the 'energy crisis' of the mid-1970s, architects modified energy-efficient planning for a conservative suburban audience. This design has all the features the market demanded, but uses only one third as much power as a conventional house.
PROMOTION AUSTRALIA

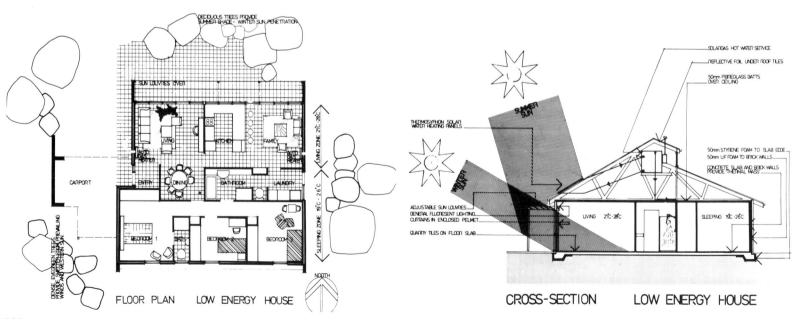

FLOOR PLAN   LOW ENERGY HOUSE

CROSS-SECTION   LOW ENERGY HOUSE

home was completed for a cost of only $29 000.

One of the points Ron stressed about his house was the thermal efficiency of 120 tonnes of concrete. To many people, the environmental impact of increased domestic fuel consumption was a more important issue than the idea of houses growing naturally out of the landscape.

The world energy crisis of the late 1970s and the resulting rise in the cost of oil had created a new consciousness of energy consumption, particularly at a domestic level. Eventually governments realised that increased public awareness of the possible benefits (and savings) of energy efficient housing could lead to reduced power consumption, and attempts were made to educate the public.

Appropriate orientation and siting, the value of insulation and correct eaves overhang became important considerations. The use of passive and active solar systems for heating, cooling, and power were explored, and many experimental ideas and designs began to emerge.

The Autonomous House, built by a group of architecture students at Sydney University, was one such experiment. The project set out to demonstrate that it was possible to build a low-cost urban house from recycled materials; one that could function independently of all services and recycle its own wastes. It was an ambitious project and not all the systems worked perfectly, but the Autonomous House stimulated a good deal of constructive thought among professionals and amateurs when it opened in 1974.

Four years later, a national competition was held by various government bodies in search of the ideal energy-efficient house. There was no single winner, but the judges selected six designs that 'combined architectural merit and conventional planning with energy saving'. Some of the designs

The Autonomous House at the University of Sydney was built of recycled materials for a cost of $700 in 1976. Its running costs were further reduced by a methane digestor, a wind generator and a solar water heater. PROMOTION AUSTRALIA

223

Manufactured in Melbourne according to a Finnish design, this 'egg' house was erected in Darwin in 1972. History does not record whether it was whisked away by Cyclone Tracy.
PROMOTION AUSTRALIA

were built as examples suitable for suburban consumption, and energy efficiency became an additional consideration for the discerning buyer.

Disaster was another force that affected many Australian homes. During the early morning of Christmas Day 1974, Darwin was struck by a lethal combination of torrential rain and wind gusts in excess of 220 kilometres per hour. In the darkness there was total chaos, as thousands of houses were literally torn apart:

A port official, Dave Walters, also moved his family into the bathroom of their government house at Moil as the cyclone approached. Bit by bit their house disintegrated until at 3 a.m. the remaining wall ripped off so he and his wife carried their children out through the raging winds to their Ford station wagon. The next-door family also lost their house at the same time so both families crammed into the Ford. For the next three hours a total of six adults and nine children clung to each other inside the vehicle. All the windows shattered except the windscreen, the car heaved and rocked, but at 6 o'clock they were still alive ...

Mr Jack Wallace, a builder who had lived in Darwin for ten years, said most of the buildings 'were smashed to pieces. There is nowhere left for people to live ... it just ripped the houses off their foundations. I made my wife and daughter lie face down on the concrete slab our house was built on. It is the only reason they survived'. [15]

With sixty-five dead, hundreds injured, and tens of thousands homeless, Darwin began to rebuild with a new awareness of the danger of cyclones. This consciousness spread through the Northern Territory and coastal Queensland, altering forever the free and easy style of houses in Australia's tropics. A 1975 government press release stated:

Darwin has adopted a completely new concept of house construction, after the cyclone which destroyed or wrecked almost every house in the city on December 25, 1974. The new approach is based on the conclusions drawn from exhaustive tests, that traditional methods of building frame houses are not acceptable in areas prone to destructive

Above: built by the Northern Territory Housing Commission, this Darwin house is designed to provide a high degree of cyclone protection as well as comfort and low energy consumption.
PROMOTION AUSTRALIA

Left: designed by the Darwin-based firm Troppo Architects, this cyclone-proof home of the 1980s combines traditional Northern Territory house-forms with efficient engineering.
TROPPO ARCHITECTS

Developed in Scandinavia, cluster housing reached Australia in the 1970s. Cartoonist Ron Tandberg may have hit on the reason for Australian home buyers' lukewarm response to this new approach to medium-density accommodation.

winds and must be replaced by the building of fully engineered houses of complete structural integrity.

Many architects produced their own version of wind-resistant architecture for northern consumption. One of the least popular concepts was a proposal by Perth architect Raymond Jones:

I am examining the possibility of a roof of polyurethane panels that will blow off in a gale, leaving a supporting frame for the wind to blow through. The idea arises from the native village principle: storms going through the thatched structures take the thatching with them but leave the basic structure more or less intact.[16]

Nothing could be more remote from thatched huts than the post-cyclone houses. With a few exceptions they were substantial and conservative, northern adaptations of the homes found in suburbs everywhere.

Architect and critic Norman Day had few kind

words to say about the state of domestic architecture in the 1970s:

The normal house Australians live in is an amalgam of dollar limit, market trends, cheapest construction allowable (which is not to say shoddy) and tiles that were at sale that week. Perhaps for special cases there is an extra bedroom with ensuite of 'plastic' olde-brick instead of the standard. Maybe flyscreens to all windows and arches out of plaster lined timber framing.

This standard 'spec' (for speculators) house is the product of a marketing industry which creates trends to suit the demands which it also creates.[17]

A study of the 'Housing Attitudes of Future Home Buyers', commissioned by the Commonwealth government in 1976, arrived at a similar conclusion:

Housing preferences are desperately unimaginative and reflect not only the pressures of price but also both a lack of awareness of anything but very

traditional styles and a desperate wish to conform to the image of a good houseprovider, especially that image held by relatives and in-laws. No one wants to be the first to go into a new style of housing . . .

There are very powerfully held beliefs about the value of ownership, the security which ownership gives, the freedom of action which ownership is seen to offer to those who now do not own homes.

The home is seen as a long term investment although resale value is important. The best thing you can do with your money is save towards a home.

Future householders expect enjoyment from gardening and renovating and would rather wait for the home that they really want than to buy a stop-gap home.

Surprisingly, over 60 per cent say they would prefer to live in the country than the city.[18]

The philosophy of the alternative lifestyle, with nostalgia for 'an old-fashioned country way of

In the 1980s, bloated land prices and consumer pressure forced revision of zoning laws in many cities, allowing grandiose villas without front fences to be built cheek-by-jowl in new suburbs.
PROMOTION AUSTRALIA

227

Soaring building costs in the last decade have inspired a search for new construction methods. These steel-framed kit homes were built by their owners for a fraction of the price of more conventional options.
NU STEEL

life', had obviously made a considerable impression on mainstream Australia, and the project home builders adjusted their sales pitch accordingly. The new range of brick veneers had names such as 'the Settler', 'Woodstock' or 'the National Homestead'. 'The Wild Colonial Boy', a typical 1984 offering from a company called Lifestyle Homes, differed from the Ranch style in name only:

Australian colonial cottage with traditional ventilated zincalume roof and front verandah. Three spacious bedrooms with walk-in robe to main and robe recesses to others. Luxury bathroom with ensuite access. Wide entry hall with feature brick planter. Spacious 23ft lounge and formal dining, with picture windows.

Frustrated at having no bush for their picture windows to overlook, many city dwellers imported the flavour of the country by creating native gardens of eucalypts, melaleucas, grevilleas and acacias, with rocks and landscaping replacing time- and water-consuming lawns.

The 1970s and 1980s also saw a revitalisation of the decaying inner-city suburbs of most capital cities. European immigrants who had arrived in Australia after World War II settled in these suburbs because they were central, unfashionable and cheap. As a result delicatessens, coffee shops, all-night cafes, and other signs of cosmopolitan street life began to appear, and these areas became much more alive and vital than the sedate middle and outer suburbs where no sound was heard after eight o'clock in the evening.

Bulk for its own sake was common in 1970s design. Rockeries and low-maintenance 'bush' gardens also came into vogue, as leisure came to mean recreation rather than gardening.
PROMOTION AUSTRALIA

Perhaps the ultimate statement in environmental sensitivity, this earth-covered building provides thermal stability and protection against bushfires while minimising impact on the landscape.
DAVID BAGGS, ECA SPACE DESIGNS

The fashion-conscious began to renovate and restore the old houses within walking distance of cities, where commuter traffic had become a major problem. Thus Carlton and Richmond in Melbourne, Paddington and the Rocks in Sydney, and Springhill in Brisbane were transformed into 'quaint and charming' areas of historic value and social desirability. Stockbrokers, lawyers and academics now proudly occupied the renovated terrace slums that had harboured the crime and poverty of the previous century. As Hal Porter said of Hobart's Battery Point:

It has become chic to live there in a village atmosphere, to retire there when a more modern house elsewhere has fulfilled earlier needs, to restore, furnish with period pieces, and cherish a dwelling — delicensed inn, workman's cottage, merchant's two-storeyed villa — of the size to fit one's purse and fancy. Curlicued barge-boards are kept in trim, Bourbon roses and white lavender grown, and a plump tortoise-shell cat kept to sit on gatepost or broad stone windowsill. It is a nerve-soothing game (not plastic lavatory seats but mahogany) as well as a way of life.[19]

In the 1980s we have become more aware that our houses have a great deal to do with our way of life. Their design, their cost, their relationship with each other and the environment are given

much more consideration than ever before.

New technology, as always, promises a better world tomorrow. Modular and prefabricated construction can drastically reduce costs. One company in Holland, for example has developed an expandable 86.6-square-metre timber house which folds up, accordion-like, into a 2.5 x 2.5 x 6-metre package. For $12000, this package can be delivered by truck to the building site, unfolded and set up on a prepared foundation in half an hour.

Underground or 'earth sheltered' housing is another possibility, combining visual harmony with incredible energy efficiency; the latest solar home designs also integrate these concepts.

At the same time the counter-reformation of

Post-Modernism has influenced the facades of some of our houses, bringing them into line with the latest imported style. And for those who don't know which way to turn, Sydney engineer Peter Aubourg has built a house that rotates at the touch of a button: living areas can follow the sun in winter and avoid it in summer. It's all a far cry from the little wattle-and-daub cottages the convicts built around Sydney Cove 200 years ago.

Modern homes are more than mere shelters; they are extremely sophisticated, complex and expensive status symbols whose importance is often exaggerated.

Reviewing the history of their development is one way of regaining a perspective.

At its best an attempt to soften the surgical inhumanity of Internationalism, the movement dubbed Post-Modernism was responsible for the pastel-painted facades on these houses in Victoria.
PROMOTION AUSTRALIA

References

Chapter 1

1. N.W. Thomas *Natives of Australia* p. 51.
2. J.C. Beaglehole (ed.) *The Endeavour journal of Joseph Banks* p. 128.
3. Robert Gouger *South Australia in 1837* p. 55.
4. Mark Heppell (ed.) *A black reality* pp. 144-45.
5. Peter Beveridge *The Aborigines of Victoria and the Riverina* p. 62.
6. E. Patterson *Walkabout* 1 Sept 1937 pp. 55-57.
7. Thomas op. cit. p. 52.
8. Joseph P. Reser *Hemisphere*.
9. Ibid.

Chapter 2

1. *Historical Records of Australia* I, part I, p. 32.
2. *Historical Records of NSW* I, part II, p. 128.
3. D. Collins *An account of the English colony* 1, p. 21.
4. *HRA* I, part I, p. 143.
5. *HRNSW* I, part II, p. 747.
6. L.F. Fitzhardinge (ed.) *Watkin Tench. Sydney's first four years* p. 195.
7. J.M. Freeland 'Elizabeth Farm' in R. Davidson (ed.) *Historic homesteads*.
8. J. Grant *The narrative of a voyage* p. 83.
9. *Sydney Gazette* Feb 1804.
10. *Sydney Gazette* Mar 1804.
11. Ibid.
12. J.B. Walker *Early Tasmania* p. 71.
13. *HRA* III, part I, p. 148.
14. W. Thornley *The adventures of an emigrant* p. 22.
15. Ibid. p. 43.
16. Ibid. p. 53

17. James Tucker *Ralph Rashleigh* pp. 104-106.
18. Scott letters 25 Sept 1825 Mitchell Library A2264.

Chapter 3

1. W. Thornley *The adventures of an emigrant* pp. 132-33.
2. Robert Gouger *South Australia in 1837* pp. 70-71.
3. J.E. Hammond *Western pioneers* p. 159.
4. E. Dianiska et al. 'Backgrounds of Melbourne brick' p. 3.
5. Gouger op. cit. p. 68.
6. E.O.G. Shann *Cattle Chosen* p. 65.
7. Gouger op. cit. p. 71.
8. E.J. Hailes *Reminiscences* p. 77.
9. Colin Kerr *'An exelent coliney'* p. 109.
10. Ibid.
11. Annie Ridley *A backward glance* p. 58.
12. Ibid. p. 57
13. Gouger op. cit. p. 125.
14. Ibid.
15. E.M. Yelland (ed.) *Colonists, copper and corn* pp. 183-84.
16. E.H. Hallack *Our townships, farms and homesteads* pp. 93-94.
17. *South Australian* 12 June 1848.
18. *Register* 26 Dec 1850.
19. Ibid.

Chapter 4

1. Antoine Fauchery *Letters from a miner* p. 24.
2. William Westall *Life in Victoria* p. 102.
3. William Howitt *Land, labour and gold* p. 159.
4. Ibid.
5. *Facts and Figures* 28 Sept 1857.
6. Westall op. cit. p. 192.

7. A. de Q. Robin (ed.) *Australian sketches* p. 80.
8. Maie Casey *An Australian story* p. 84.
9. Mrs Charles Meredith *My home in Tasmania* pp. 116-118.
10. Ibid. pp. 155, 156.
11. Ibid. p. 367.
12. Joan Starr *Pioneering New England* pp. 18, 19.
13. Hugh McCrae (ed.) *Georgiana's journal* p. 227.
14. F. Lancelot *Australia as it is* p. 118.
15. *The Australian enquirer* pp. 192-204.
16. Eve Pownall *Mary of Maranoa* p. 171.
17. *South Australian Register* July 1908.
18. G.S. Harman (ed.) *Squatters, miners and scholars* p. 78.
19. Hugh Anderson *Time out of mind* p. 16.
20. George William Easton 'Reminiscences', in Peter Mercer 'From Raj to rustic'.
21. Pownall op. cit. p. 64.
22. George Fletcher Moore *Diary of ten years eventful life* p. 53.
23. Harman op. cit. p. 78.
24. Alfred Joyce *A homestead history* p. 51.
25. Charles Ferguson *The experiences of a forty-niner* p. 469.
26. *The Australian enquirer* p. 204.
27. Rachel Henning *The letters of Rachel Henning* p. 62.
28. Anne Baxter *Memories of the past*.
29. Mary Durack *Kings in grass castles*.
30. Alexander Harris *Settlers and convicts* p. 159.
31. Henning op. cit. p. 53.

Chapter 5

1. Charles Mundy *Sydney town 1846-51* p. 31.
2. Ibid. p. 32.

3   Ibid.
4   Derek Whitelock *Adelaide 1836-1976* p. 179.
5   Joseph Elliott *Our home in Australia* p. 46.
6   Ibid. p. 40
7   Ibid. p. 60.
8   Ibid. p. 61.
9   Ibid. p. 64.
10   Ibid. p. 76.
11   Barry Groom & Warren Wickman *Sydney — the 1850s* p. 47.
12   Ibid. p. 74.
13   Mary Banks *Memories of pioneer days* pp. 42-43.
14   Charles Allen *A visit to Queensland* p. 110.
15   Ibid. p. 162.
16   George Ellis *Modern practical carpentry* p. 270.
17   William Howitt *Land, labour and gold* p. 159.
18   D.E. Kelsey *The shackle* p. 72.
19   *Historical Records of Australia* 1, 26, p. 374.
20   *Queenslander* 5 June 1875.
21   J. Moffat letterbook 1883-84, p. 82.
22   M. Ryan *Newsletter of the RAHS* Oct 1975 p. 7.
23   T.P.L. Weitemeyer *Missing friends* p. 92.
24   Allen op. cit. p. 163.
25   E.S. Leyland et al. *Working drawings and designs.*

Chapter 6

1   Nehemiah Bartley *Opals and agates* p. 296.
2   James Inglis *Our Australian cousins* p. 145.
3   Ibid.
4   R.E.N. Twopeny *Town life in Australia* p. 45.
5   John Buncle *Experiences of a Victorian manufacturer.*
6   H. Joseland in *Building and Engineering Journal* 13 Aug 1891 p. 63.
7   Twopeny op. cit. p. 31.

8   Ibid. p. 38.
9   Dennis O'Donovan 'Art in building — construction' Industrial & Technological Museum lectures 1873.
10   Twopeny op. cit. p. 31.
11   Ibid. p. 36.
12   Harry Hodge *The Hill End story* p. 148.
13   J.M. Freeland *Architecture in Australia* pp. 190, 191.
14   George Farwell *Squatter's castle* p. 283.
15   Alan Brissenden (ed.) *Henry Lawson's Australia* pp. 82, 83.
16   Steele Rudd in Michael Cannon *Life in the country* p. 147.
17   A.B. Facey *A fortunate life* p. 19.
18   E.J. Banfield *Confessions of a beachcomber.*
19   Edward S. Sorenson *Life in the Australian backblocks* p. 9.
20   Ibid. p. 14.
21   Peter Forrest 'Old buildings in western Queensland' *Sphere* Oct 1979 p. 26.
22   Sorenson op. cit. p. 10.
23   D.E. Kelsey *The shackle* p. 108.

Chapter 7

1   Lucien Henry in the *Australasian*, reprinted in *Australian Builder and Contractor's News* 28 Feb 1891.
2   E. Wunderlich *Our work* p. 37.
3   Robert Haddon *Australian architecture* p. 44.
4   E.C. Buley *Australian life in town and country.*
5   J.S. Gawler *A roof over my head* pp. 48, 49.
6   F. Walton *Infancy and development of linoleum floorcloth* p. 25.
7   *Plant Analysis* 57 1905 p. 13.
8   *XXth century cooking and home decoration* pp. 303, 304.
9   Mrs Aeneas Gunn *We of the Never Never* p. 54.
10   Ibid. p. 53.
11   Dorothy Roysland *A pioneer family* pp. 16-18.

12   Ibid. pp. 19-20.
13   Ibid. p. 19.
14   Haddon op. cit. pp. 195, 196.
15   E.D. Daniel *Grandfather was a Maldon pioneer* p. 38.
16   M. McAdoo *When Grandma was just a girl* p. 93.
17   Gawler op. cit. pp. 53, 54.
18   R.A. Briggs *Bungalows and country residences* p. 39.
19   *Building (Australia)* 15 June 1908.
20   George Foletta *Woven threads* pp. 47, 48.

Chapter 8

1   Stanley Diss Oral history interview 24961 Battye Library.
2   Elsie Firth 'A letter to my grand-daughter' p. 3.
3   'The futurist home' *Home* June 1921 p. 28.
4   *Real Property Annual* June 1921 p. 75.
5   *Walkabout* 1 Sept 1939 p. 57.
6   *Gold Coast Bulletin* 5 Sept 1985 p. 32.
7   *Home* Jan 1927 p. 62.
8   D.H. Lawrence *Kangaroo* p. 5.
9   Ibid. p. 350.
10   Mary Vera Adams *No stranger in paradise* p. 151.
11   *Home* 1 July 1927 p. 26.
12   Ibid. p. 42.
13   Edna Walling *Cottage and garden* p. 3.
14   *Australia's yesterdays* p. 81.
15   J.S. Gawler *A roof over my head* pp. 54, 55.
16   *Australian Home Beautiful* 1 Sept 1938 p. 30.
17   Interview with author Melbourne 1985.
18   *Australian Home Beautiful* 2 Jan 1939 p. 16.

Chapter 9

1   J.S. Gawler *A roof over my head* p. 56.
2   *Australian House & Garden* Feb 1949 pp. 26, 27.
3   *Australian Home Beautiful* May 1948 p. 17.

4 Leonard Bullen *Selected home designs* p. 7.

5 *Build your own home* p. 7.

6 Interview with author Adelaide 1983.

7 Interview with author Adelaide 1983.

8 *Australian Women's Weekly* Mar 1951 p. 27.

9 Felicity St John Moore *Vassilieff* p. 72.

10 Interview with author Melbourne 1983.

11 Interview with author Melbourne 1983.

12 David Malouf *12 Edmonstone Street* pp. 49, 50.

13 *Australian House & Garden* Jan 1952 p. 32.

14 Ibid.

15 Interview with author Melbourne 1985.

16 Interview with author Melbourne 1985.

17 Cyril Pearl *So you want to buy a house?* pp. 4-6.

18 *Australian House & Garden* Jan 1958 p. 25.

Chapter 10

1 *Australian House & Garden* Oct 1961 p. 16.

2 Robin Boyd *The Australian ugliness* p. 32.

3 *Australian House & Garden* Oct 1961 p. 18.

4 Ibid.

5 *Architecture in Australia* Dec 1963 p. 80.

6 *Australian Home Beautiful* Mar 1968 p. 6.

7 Ibid. June 1967 p. 10.

8 Craig McGregor *Profile of Australia* p. 122.

9 *Australian Home Beautiful* April 1968 p. 12.

10 Ibid. p. 3.

11 *Homefront* 1977.

12 Alistair Knox *Living in the environment* p. 140.

13 Ibid. p. viii.

14 *Age* 30 July 1977.

15 Alan Stretton *The furious days* pp. 18, 19.

16 Australian Information Service 1 Aug 1975.

17 Norman Day *Modern houses Melbourne* p. 18.

18 David Maddocks *Exploring the housing attitudes of future home buyers* pp. 5, 21.

19 Hal Porter in *Seven cities of Australia* pp. 49, 50.

Acknowledgments

The author and publishers would like to thank the individuals and organisations listed below for permission to reproduce copyright material:

The J.S. Battye Library of West Australian History for photographs on pp. 5 (9061P), 16 (29203P), 45 (6890P), 46 (5002P), 47 (26420P, 26510P), 48 (2207P), 49 (26426P, 26387P), 57 (5281B/67), 72 (1139B/83), 115 (27970P), 116 (27969P), 125 (9095P), 126 (29856P), 127 (1139B/33), 135 (9159B), 139 (5281B/8), 144 (6183P), 149 (6349P), 150 (20810P), 151 (66997P), 154 (9062P), 156 (12732P), 160 (6183P), 164 (12624P), 165 (12734P), 166 (12733P), 175 (816B/B2887), 180 (13180P, 13159P), 181 (13157P, 13365P), 182 (19656P); photo reference numbers are in brackets.

Photographs on pp. 120 and 150 courtesy the trustees, Museum of Applied Arts and Sciences (Power House Museum).

Extracts on p. 17 from Mark Heppell (ed.) *A black reality* courtesy the Australian Institute of Aboriginal Studies Canberra; pp. 34, 35, 41 from W. Thornley *The adventures of an emigrant in Van Diemen's Land,* p. 51 from Colin Kerr 'A exelent coliney', pp. 65-7 from Joan Starr *Pioneering New England,* and pp. 151-2 from Dorothy Roysland *A pioneer family on the Murray River* courtesy Rigby; pp. 43-5 from E.O.G. Shann *Cattle Chosen* courtesy Oxford University Press Oxford; p. 63 from Maie Casey *An Australian story* courtesy Michael Joseph Ltd London; pp. 69, 73 from Eve Pownall *Mary of Maranoa* courtesy Melbourne University Press; pp. 91-3, and illustrations on pp. 91, 92, from Joseph Elliott *Our home in Australia* courtesy Brian Elliott; p. 113 from J.M. Freeland *Architecture in Australia* courtesy Mrs Kathleen Freeland; p. 127 from A.B. Facey *A fortunate life* courtesy Penguin Books Australia Ltd; pp. 144-6, 155, 174, 185 from J.S. Gawler *A roof over my head* courtesy Mrs Ruth Gawler; p. 155 from M. McAdoo *When Grandma was just a girl* courtesy Lansdowne; pp. 155-9 from George Foletta *Woven threads* courtesy Bruce Foletta; pp. 187-9, 200, 202, 207, 209, 210-11 from *Australian House & Garden* and p. 191 from *Australian Women's Weekly* courtesy Australian Consolidated Press; pp. 197-8 from David Malouf *12 Edmonstone Street* courtesy Curtis Brown (Aust.) Pty Ltd; pp. 209-10 from Robin Boyd *The Australian Ugliness* courtesy Longman Cheshire Pty Ltd Melbourne; p. 212 from *Architecture in Australia* courtesy Architecture Media Australia Pty Ltd; pp. 215-17 from Craig McGregor *Profile of Australia* courtesy Hodder & Stoughton Ltd London; pp. 217-18 from *Homefront* courtesy Enterprise Advertising Adelaide; p. 224 from Alan Stretton *The furious days* courtesy William Collins; p. 230 from Hal Porter 'Hobart' in *Seven cities of Australia* (John Ferguson 1978) courtesy John F. Porter.

Every effort has been made to determine and locate the copyright owners. In the case of any omissions the publishers will be pleased to make suitable acknowledgment in future editions.

Bibliography

Adams, Vera Mary *No stranger in paradise* Sydney 1976.

Allen, Charles *A visit to Queensland and her goldfields* London 1870.

Anderson, Hugh *Time out of mind* Melbourne 1974.

Apsley, Lord & Lady *The amateur settlers* London 1927.

Australia's yesterdays Sydney 1974.

Baggs, Sydney, Joan & David *Australian earth-covered buildings* Sydney 1985.

Baird, John *By design* Melbourne 1984.

Banfield, E.J. *Confessions of a beachcomber* (1908) rev. edn London 1980.

Banks, Mary *Memories of pioneer days in Queensland* London 1927.

Bartley, Nehemiah *Opals and agates* Brisbane 1892.

Beaglehole, J.C. (ed.) *The Endeavour journal of Joseph Banks* (2 vols) Sydney 1961.

Bell, Peter *Timber and iron: houses in north Queensland mining settlements, 1861-1920* Brisbane 1984.

Berry, D.W. & S.H. Guilbert *Pioneer building techniques in South Australia* Adelaide 1981.

Beveridge, Peter *The Aborigines of Victoria and the Riverina* Melbourne 1889.

Boyd, Robin *Australia's home: its origins, builders and occupiers* Melbourne 1968
—— *The Australian ugliness* Melbourne 1963.

Briggs, R.A. *Bungalows and country residences* London 1891.

Brissenden, Alan (ed.) *Henry Lawson's Australia* Sydney 1979.

Buley, E.C. *Australian life in town and country* Sydney 1910.

Buncle, John *Experience of a Victorian manufacturer* Melbourne 1887.

Cannon, Michael *Australia in the Victorian age* (3 vols): *Who's master? Who's man?* Melbourne 1971; *Life in the country* Melbourne 1973; *Life in the cities* Melbourne 1975.

Casey, Maie *An Australian story* Melbourne 1957.

Collins, D. *An account of the English colony in New South Wales* (2 vols, 1798 & 1802) republished Sydney 1975.

Cox, Phillip, John Freeland & Wesley Stacey *Rude timber buildings in Australia* Sydney 1980.

Cuffley, Peter *Cottage gardens in Australia* Melbourne 1984.

Daniel, E.D. *Grandfather was a Maldon pioneer* Kew, Victoria 1963.

Davidson, R. (ed.) *Historic homesteads of Australia* Sydney 1969.

Day, Norman *Modern houses Melbourne* Melbourne 1976.

de Q. Robin, A. (ed.) *Australian sketches. The journals of Francis Perry* Melbourne 1976.

Dianiska, E. et al. 'Backgrounds of Melbourne brick' B. Architecture report University of Melbourne 1959.

Durack, Mary *Kings in grass castles* London 1959.

Dutton, Geoffrey *The squatters* Melbourne 1985.

Elliott, Joseph *Our home in Australia: a description of cottage life in 1860* Sydney 1984.

Ellis, George *Modern practical carpentry for the use of workmen, builders, architects and engineers* London 1915.

Evans, Ian *Restoring old houses* Sydney 1979.
—— *The Australian home* Sydney 1983.
—— *The Federation house* Sydney 1985.

Eyland, E.S., F. Lightbody, & R.S. Burn *Working drawings and designs in architecture and building* Edinburgh 1866.

Facey, A.B. *A fortunate life* Melbourne 1981.

Farwell, George *Squatters castle* Melbourne 1973.

Fauchery, Antoine *Letters from a miner in Australia* Melbourne 1965 (trans. *Lettres d'un mineur en Australie* Paris 1857).

Ferguson, Charles *The experiences of a forty-niner during thirty-four years' residence in California and Australia* Ohio 1888.

Firth, Elsie 'A letter to my grand-daughter' undated ms Battye Library.

Fitzhardinge, L.F. (ed.) *Watkin Tench. Sydney's first four years: being a reprint of 'A narrative of the expedition to Botany Bay' and 'A complete account of the settlement at Port Jackson'* Sydney 1961.

Foletta, George *Woven threads* Melbourne 1975.

Forge, Suzanne *Victorian splendour: Australian interior decoration 1837-1901* Melbourne 1981.

Fraser, Hugh & Ray Joyce *The Federation house* Sydney 1986.

Freeland, J.M. *Architecture in Australia: a history* Melbourne 1968.

Gawler, J.S. *A roof over my head* Melbourne 1963.

Gouger, Robert *South Australia in 1837* London 1838.

Grant, J. *The narrative of a voyage of discovery performed in his majesty's vessel The Lady Nelson, etc.* London 1803.

Groom, Barry & Warren Wickman (eds) *Sydney — the 1850s. The lost collections* Sydney 1982.

Gunn, Mrs Aeneas *We of the Never Never* Sydney 1982.

Haddon, Robert *Australian architecture* Melbourne 1905.

Hailes, E.J. *Reminiscences* Adelaide 1893.

Hallack, E.H. *Our townships, farms and homesteads* Sydney 1908.

Hammond, J.E. *Western pioneers* Perth 1980.

Harman, G.S. (ed.) *Squatters, miners and scholars* Armidale NSW 1963.

Harris, Alexander *Settlers and convicts, or recollections of sixteen years' labour in the Australian backwoods by an emigrant mechanic* London 1847.

Harris, Phillip & Adrian Welke *Punkahs and pith helmets: good principles of tropical house design* Darwin 1982.

Henning, Rachel (D. Adams ed.) *The letters of Rachel Henning* Sydney 1963.

Heppell, Mark (ed.) *A black reality —Aboriginal camps and housing in remote Australia* Canberra 1979.

Hodge, Harry *The Hill End story* (3 vols) Sydney 1964.

Howitt, William *Land, labour and gold; (or two years in Victoria).* London 1855.

Inglis, James *Our Australian cousins* London 1850.

Joyce, Alfred (G.F. James ed.) *A homestead history* Melbourne 1949.

Kelsey, D.E. (Ira Nesdale ed.) *The shackle: a story of the far north Australian bush* Adelaide 1975.

Kerr, Colin *'A exelent coliney'* Melbourne 1981.

Knox, Alistair *Living in the environment* Eltham, Vic 1975.

Lancelot, F. *Australia as it is: its settlements, farms and goldfields* (2 vols) London 1852.

Lawrence, D.H. *Kangaroo* London 1932.

McAdoo, M. *When Grandma was just a girl* Sydney 1983.

McCrae, Hugh (ed.) *Georgiana's journal* Sydney 1934.

McGregor, Craig *Profile of Australia* London 1966.

Maddocks, David *Exploring the attitudes of future Australian homebuyers in four Australian cities* Canberra 1976.

Malouf, David *12 Edmonstone Street* London 1985.

Mercer, Peter 'From Raj to rustic: a history of the Easton family' unpublished ms (no date).

Meredith, Mrs Charles *My home in Tasmania or nine years in Australia* New York 1883.

Moore, George Fletcher *Diary of ten years eventful life of an early settler in Western Australia* Perth 1978.

Mundy, Charles *Sydney Town 1846-51* (originally published as 'Our Antipodes' London 1852).

Pearl, Cyril *So you want to buy a house?* Melbourne 1961.

Pownall, Eve *Mary of Maranoa* Melbourne 1959.

Read, Herbert *The politics of the unpolitical* London 1943.

Ridley, Annie *A backward glance. The story of John Ridley, a pioneer* London 1904.

Roysland, Dorothy *A pioneer family on the Murray River* Adelaide 1977.

Rudd, Steele *On our selection* Sydney 1899.

Rudofsky, B. *Architecture without architects. A short introduction to non-pedigreed architecture* London 1964.

St John Moore, Felicity *Vassilieff and his art* Melbourne 1982.

Seven cities of Australia Sydney 1978.

Shann, E.O.G. *Cattle Chosen* Perth 1926.

Sorenson, Edward S. *Life in the Australian backblocks* London 1911.

Starr, Joan *Pioneering New England* Adelaide 1978.

Stone, Derrick & Donald S. Garden *Squatters and settlers* Melbourne 1978.

Stretton, Alan *The furious days* Sydney 1976.

Sumner, Ray *Settlers and habitat in tropical Queensland* Townsville 1974.

Thomas, N.W. *Natives of Australia* Melbourne 1906.

Thornley, W. (John Mills ed.) *The adventures of an emigrant in Van Diemen's Land* Adelaide 1973.

Tucker, James *Ralph Rashleigh* Sydney 1962.

Twopeny, R.E.N. *Town life in Australia* London 1883.

Walker, J.B. *Early Tasmania* Hobart 1963.

Walker, Murray *Pioneer crafts of early Australia* Melbourne 1978.

Walling, Edna *Cottage and garden in Australia* Melbourne 1947.

Walton, F. *Infancy and development of linoleum floorcloth* London 1925.

Weitemeyer, T.P.L. *Missing friends; being the adventures of a Danish emigrant in Queensland, 1871-1880* London 1892.

Westall, William *Life in Victoria* Melbourne 1873.

Whitelock, Derek *Adelaide 1836-1976* Brisbane 1977.

Williams, W.H. *Memories of the past by a lady in Australia* Melbourne 1873.

Wilson, Granville & Peter Sands *Building a city* Melbourne 1981.

Wunderlich, E. *Our work* Sydney 1910.

Yelland, E.M. (ed.) *Colonists, copper and corn in the colony of South Australia 1850-51, by an old colonist* Melbourne 1970.

Young, G., A. Aeuchkens, A. Green & S. Nikias *Lobethal 'Valley of Praise'* Adelaide 1983.

Young, G., I. Harmstorf, L. Brasse & A. Marsden *Hahndorf* (2 vols) Adelaide 1981.

Index

239